Lessons of Peace and Development

Gurage Entrepreneurship in Ethiopia

Daniel Teferra

UNIVERSITY PRESS OF AMERICA,® INC
Lanham • Boulder • New York • Toronto • Plymouth, UK

Copyright © 2008 by
Daniel Teferra

University Press of America,® Inc.
4501 Forbes Boulevard
Suite 200
Lanham, Maryland 20706
UPA Acquisitions Department (301) 459-3366

Estover Road
Plymouth PL6 7PY
United Kingdom

All rights reserved
Printed in the United States of America
British Library Cataloging in Publication Information Available

Library of Congress Control Number: 2007943310
ISBN-13: 978-0-7618-4005-3 (paperback : alk. paper)
ISBN-10: 0-7618-4005-2 (paperback : alk. paper)

Cover photo: A Silte house

∞™ The paper used in this publication meets the minimum requirements of American National Standard for Information Sciences—Permanence of Paper for Printed Library Materials, ANSI Z39.48—1984

For Gurage Entrepreneurs

"The Gurage do not steal or cheat. They do not beg. They like work. If one tries to beg, they get together and help him out to be a productive member of society. They are fair and respectable people. They respect their culture and this has given them self-confidence."

The late Ato Debebe Habte Yohannes
The Pioneer of Private Banking in Ethiopia

Contents

Preface		vii
1	History of Economic Development	1
	The Developed World	1
	Economic Development and Africa	4
	International Development Assistance	5
	Ethiopia's Formation and Economic Development	7
2	Entrepreneurship and Economic Development	40
	Origins of Entrepreneurship	40
	Historical Background of the Gurage	42
	Gurage Work Ethic and Frugality	46
	Gurage Cooperation	54
3	Summary and Conclusion	63
Appendix I		75
Appendix II		79
Appendix III		81
Bibliography		83
Index		85

Preface

The blessing of peace and development may be confined to limited areas of the earth's surface, but one can find nuclei of industrious groups making major contributions to economic development in different parts of the world. Historically, for instance, certain enterprising communities in Africa, such as the Luo of Kenya, Ibo of Nigeria, or the Gurage of Ethiopia have, through their customary drive, worked hard and created wealth for themselves and their societies. There is, however, very little known about these communities. First, they are denied the social status commensurate with their economic success in their own societies. Second, the West and its development organizations, emphasizing only external factors, such as inflow of capital ignore indigenous institutions of development.

In Ethiopia, the Gurage are well known for their entrepreneurial attitude. However, no serious study of Gurage entrepreneurship has been done. This work is, therefore, the first attempt to fill this gap. There are some works on different aspects of the Gurage. One of the earlier studies is by William Shack, entitled *The Gurage: A People of the Enset Culture* (1966). Another informative book on the Gurage society is by Gebreyesus Haile Mariam, entitled *The Gurage and their Culture* (1991). Several other useful studies on the Gurage have also been produced by Tesfa Gebreyes, Worku Nida, Denberu Alemu et. al., Getinet Assefa, Shimelis Bonsa, and others. The author has benefited greatly from all these works. A recent study by Taye Mengistae, sponsored by the World Bank, about African ethnic businesses concludes that Gurage-owned manufacturing businesses perform better than those owned by other major or minor groups. The study argues that this success is due to the larger size and faster growth rate of Gurage businesses, although Gurage business owners are the least educated. The study further states that "the observed effect of ethnicity could be indicative of inter-group differences in unmeasured ability." However, it does not show what it calls "inter-group differences in unmeasured ability."[1]

The Gurage are proficient entrepreneurs and sensitive to the efficient use of time and resources. They shun violence and resolve their differences through peaceful means. They cooperate among themselves and mentor one another. By controlling violence, they have been able to direct their energies and resources towards productive purposes. The Gurage contribute disproportionately to economic development in Ethiopia. They make up about 4 percent of the Ethiopian population, yet they account for 55 to 60 percent of the business activities in Addis Ababa alone (see Table 2.1).

The Gurage are different in their attitude from the rest of the Ethiopian society. They have a strong work ethic. They save their money and invest in productive activities. They are peaceful and cooperative. They work well with the other groups. Yet the Gurage are not racially different from the other ethnic groups of Ethiopia. They have had no colonial or other type of contact with the Western societies. How then did the Gurage acquire an entrepreneurial behavior of work ethic, frugality and cooperation while the other ethnic groups did not, even though they are racially the same? The main purpose of this study, in general terms, is to explore the answer to this question by taking a closer look at the specific history and socioeconomic institutions that have shaped and sustained the Gurage work ethic, frugality and cooperation over time.

This study has three major parts. The first part discusses the development history of the now advanced societies, Africa's development experiment as well as Ethiopia's formation and development experience. The second section examines various theories about the origins of entrepreneurship, the history of the Gurage and Gurage entrepreneurial attitude. The third part will give summary and conclusion.

This is an independent study and the information has been collected through library research as well as interviews and surveys conducted by the author in Ethiopia. In preparing this work I have received assistance from a number of wonderful people. I would especially like to thank Ato Bogale Demissie, who kindly gave his time in helping me collect information through interviewing elders (wise men), business people and other members of the Gurage community in the Markato, the central market, in Addis Ababa.

I am immensely thankful to Kenyazmach Teka Egeno, the late Likatiguhan Getachew Debela, the late Ato Dembal Shai, Ato.Tamene Shalemo, Ato Abebe Bekele, Ato Gebreyesus Haile Mariam and Ato Mebratu Lemma for their time and generosity in providing me with valuable information about the Gurage society and its history. I am greatly indebted to Ato Gizaw Zergaw for sharing his valuable knowledge of the Gurage society and business acumen. I would like to thank deeply Woizero Haregewoin Asfaw for her valuable information on the Gurage family and Gurage women. I would like to thank Ato Legesse Zerihun for his generous hospitality and kind assistance. I am grateful to him and Ato Lemma Habtegiorgis for sharing with me their entrepreneurial experiences and for their insightful information.

Many thanks are owed to the library staff of the Institute of Ethiopian Studies, Addis Ababa University. In particular, I would like to thank Woizero Birhane Gebre Mariam, Woizero Felekech Abera, Ato Bayu Kebede and Ato Mesfin Ayenachew. A very special gratitude is due to Ato Darfeta Shawa for his unselfish cooperation and generous assistance during my work at the Library. I am deeply grateful to him for his help during my visit to the Gurage countryside. I would also like to thank the very helpful and cooperative staff of the Bete Gurage Cultural Center in Addis Ababa. I owe a debt of gratitude to Professors Teshome Abebe and Theodore M. Vestal for their review and gracious comments. I would also like to thank my long time friend Ato Getachew Ashinne for his kindness and generous support during my stay in Addis Ababa. Finally, My thanks go to Dr. Catherine Rasmussen and Samra Ellen Teferra for their editorial assistance. Last but not least, I would like to thank Teferra Daniel Teferra for his insightful suggestions at the inception of this study and for his technical assistance with the computer production of the manuscript.

Daniel Teferra
Madison, Wisconsin, U.S.A., 2007

NOTE

1. Taye Mengistae, "Indigenous Ethnicity and Entrepreneurial Success in Africa, Some Evidence from Ethiopia," (The World Bank, Development Research Group, Macroeconomics and Growth, January 2001).

Chapter One

History of Economic Development

THE DEVELOPED WORLD

Great Britain first achieved economic development as the Industrial Revolution transformed the country between 1760 and 1830 in ways previously unknown. Then in the last half of the nineteenth century a number of progressive economies in Western Europe and elsewhere followed Britain's example.

The spread of technical knowledge from Great Britain and the part played by British entrepreneurs, capital, managers and skilled labor in the industrialization of France, Germany, Belgium and Switzerland were significant. In other countries, such as, Sweden, economic development was less influenced by Britain and more self-generated. Australia, New Zealand, and Canada were among the progressive economies that had developed by the late nineteenth century. The development of Germany and the United States, in particular, was so impressive that they rivaled Britain's industrial supremacy by the 1890s.[1] Japan also became an industrial power by the end of the nineteenth century. British capital and entrepreneurial influence also brought great achievements in South Africa and Argentina.

The Industrial Revolution that began in Great Britain by no means guaranteed the immediate establishment of the factory system in the rest of the world. In fact, the British sought to prevent the dissemination abroad of the details of the new inventions. This British effort possibly accounted for a time lag of some years in the introduction of the new machines to the United States. On the other hand, the new techniques could be imported when American entrepreneurs with sufficient capital became aware of the possibilities of employing them profitably. The prohibition against exporting British technology also served the United States as a powerful spur to develop its own industrial revolution. At first, the United States imported machines or copied them from English models, but then developed independently higher quality machines for its manufactures.[2]

In all these countries, the modern nation-state promoted the interests of the entrepreneurial society. It turned land over to the peasantry and lifted restrictions on free movement of people and goods. The modern nation-state established and enforced the legal equality of all individuals, groups and interests of society. It gave everybody the legal freedom to choose his/her trade or occupation and accumulate wealth and enrich himself/herself. It encouraged agricultural development and manufacturing and engaged in public enterpreneurship. The modern nation-state supported private entrepreneurship and created a unity of purpose and social cohesiveness by directing the energies of the society to a national economy and international competition.

Some variations could be observed in the role that government played in the now industrialized societies. In Great Britain, the United States of America, France and Germany, an innovative entrepreneurial class led economic development with minimum government intervention. In Germany and France, government-sponsored development efforts exceeded those in Great Britain and the United States of America. In Japan, on the other hand, government that possessed entrepreneurial talents and leadership of quality in its ranks led the business of economic development. Japan was able to achieve economic development by absorbing rapidly the backlog of available technologies and the flow of new ideas.

In the first half of the twentieth century, Russia (under the Soviet system) joined the ranks of leading industrial countries. Economic development had already been underway in Russia in the 1890s, brining to life modern coal, iron and heavy engineering industries followed by the spread of technology to steel fabrication, chemicals and electricity. There was also substantial surplus in agriculture. Although Russia was the least developed European power in the late nineteenth century, it was a developed power nonetheless, competing economically with some European states and possessing some modern industries with well equipped factories that used the most up-to-date Western models.[3]

The Soviet development model that was once hailed as a unique experience in human history is now gone. Although the system initially helped promote a rate of economic growth more rapid than would likely be possible in a market economy, it failed to meet the changing economic needs of the country in the 1970s and 1980s.[4] The Soviet experiment illustrates that command growth is possible for short periods, even decades, but cannot be sustained for a long period of time.

Another latecomer that employed the command growth model is the People's Republic of China. Here too, the command growth model played an important role, but centuries of accumulated knowledge provided the development nucleus for assuring further growth.

China, of course, did not achieve the technological and scientific levels reached by the West and Japan in the late nineteenth century. Several factors contributed to this failure. Foreign imperialist intervention was one of them. There were also internal factors, such as China's conservatism, the decline of scientific inquiry, lack of substantial investment capital and a tremendous population explosion, accompanied by a very low purchasing power, which failed to provide a stimulus to production.[5]

Prior to the Industrial Revolution in the West, China's material culture was by no means inferior to that of any other country. Immensely important changes, refinements and creative contributions to human culture had continued in China for centuries. In the thirteenth century, China reached a level of scientific knowledge that had not been approached in the West. The Chinese civilization made original advances in the arts, science, industry and agriculture, and Europe borrowed many of these inventions. Despite dynastic interregnums, all this knowledge was never lost, but compounded itself cumulatively, making Chinese industrial revolution inevitable in the end.[6]

From 1965 to 1990 South Korea, Taiwan, Hong Kong and Singapore, popularly nicknamed the Four Tigers, led the list of newly industrialized countries. The list included Brazil, Mexico, Israel, the Philippines, Thailand, Indonesia and Malaysia.

The Four Tigers are often cited as outstanding cases of poor countries transforming themselves in a short period of time. South Korea and Taiwan have many similarities. They both enjoyed advantages from Japanese colonization in the first part of the twentieth century. South Korea emphasized education on its own. Aid from the United States was intelligently used, especially in building an infrastructure of roads, railways, ports, communications, electric generation and a power grid. Land reform and rural manufacturing were used to narrow income gaps. Subsidies, tax reductions and preferential access to the big U.S. market helped to overcome infant industry problems and promote a successful export-led development.[7]

Towards the late 1960s, largely under U.S. pressure, a general rethinking occurred in Taiwan. Price and exchange controls were dismantled. Military expenditure was reduced in proportion to both GNP and total government expenditure. Officials turned away from government initiative as the spearhead for development and relied on private entrepreneurs and the market. Multinational corporations were welcomed and government funds were directed more toward agriculture and infrastructure.[8]

ECONOMIC DEVELOPMENT AND AFRICA

Not much was known about Africa at the time of the first Industrial Revolution in the eighteenth century. One hundred years later in the nineteenth century, Africa was still little more than a coastline, a coastline not representative of the interior. There was no demand for the new European technology, nor was there an entrepreneurial class that could see profit in internalizing the new technology. "Hunting for elephants or captives did not induce in Africa a demand for any technology other than firearms. Africa's external trade relations were either destructive as slavery was, or at best purely extractive, like ivory hunting and cutting cam wood trees."[9]

South Africa, on the other hand, long penetrated by European settlers, was the exception. By the late nineteenth century, South Africa was already a progressive economy, capable of internalizing modern technology. The exploitation of cheap Black labor and the discovery of the world's richest gold-bearing reef on the Witwaterstrand, where the city of Johannesburg stood, were major benefits. South Africa now possesses a well-developed market economy, sophisticated infrastructure and a relatively large White population with a strong entrepreneurial class. It is very rich in natural resources, a major supplier of precious metals to the industrialized countries and a world leader in tourism. South Africa has strong trade and investment links with the industrialized societies of the world. More than 40 percent of Africa's share of world trade comes from South Africa.[10] South Africa is a net exporter of food and has trade, transport and employment links with the entire southern African region; consequently, it plays a leading role in the regional economy, accounting for about 75 percent of the region's gross domestic product.

However, because of the legacy of apartheid, South Africa's modern and sophisticated first world (mainly Whites and Indians) comprises not more than 30 percent of the population. The majority of the Black population is still in the third world ironically living in a relatively better condition than the populations in other African countries thanks to a well-developed wage economy.

South Africa's development experience does not fit the African mold. Economic development efforts actually began in the rest of Africa only in the 1960s and most of the Continent is still untouched by it. Africa may not boast progressive economies yet, but there have been some useful experiences worth mentioning. In West Africa, the development of Cote d'Ivoire (Ivory Coast) was hailed as an exemplary endeavor. When Cote d'Ivoire gained its independence in 1960, its per capita income was only about $70. By 1976, the per capita income of Cote d'Ivoire increased almost nine times to $610.[11] Cote d'Ivoire made its advances by concentrating on primary product exports despite the Prebisch model that views export of primary commodities as the main cause for a persistent, long term deterioration of the terms of trade of a developing country.[12]

Cote d'Ivoire was able to raise its exports of cocoa by four times and coffee by five times in 25 years from 1950 to 1975. By 1985, Cote d'Ivoire was the world's number one exporter of cocoa and the third largest exporter of coffee. During most of this period, earnings from exports were growing 10 percent annually. From 1970 to 1982, the gross national product growth rate was 6 percent annually. Although the growth rate was less than that of the Four Tigers, Cote d'Ivoire performed very well compared to the rest of sub-Saharan Africa where economic performance was generally poor.[13]

Cote d'Ivoire's success during this time was attributed to a policy of higher prices for enterprising farmers, to which they responded by increasing their production. Taxes on exports were reduced and foreign exchange earnings increased to finance investment in infrastructure, and agricultural development.[14]

In the early 1980s, Cote d'Ivoire was hit by the debt crisis that engulfed many developing countries. The failure of the rains that also affected much of Africa ruined the coffee crop and dried up the rivers that powered the hydroelectric facilities, thereby reducing the electricity supply and industrial production. All this caused per capita growth to slip, but in 1985 and 1986, Cote d'Ivoire rebounded—evidence that the economy was not only successful but resilient.[15]

In East Africa, Kenya's post-independence development record was unusually good. Compared to other countries in the region, Kenya had a stronger infrastructure, left behind by the British. Kenya's real gross domestic product increased by 6.8 percent on average between 1965 and 1978. Even with a population growth rate of 3.5 percent per year, the per capita gross domestic product was growing by 3.3 percent.

In contrast, Tanzania followed the path of socialism and the results were not promising. Between 1965 and 1978, Tanzania's average growth rate was 4.8 percent. With a relatively smaller population growth rate of 2.7 percent, Tanzania's per capita gross domestic product grew by only 1.1 percent.[16]

INTERNATIONAL DEVELOPMENT ASSISTANCE

After the end of the Second World War, development specialists divided the world into developed and less developed countries on the basis of per capita income. Then foreign loans and aid began to flow from the developed to the less developed countries through all sorts of bilateral and multilateral arrangements. However, several decades later the developing countries of the world, most of them in Africa, had become poorer and more dependent than ever on foreign loans and aid. The leaders of these countries, in fact, viewed the flow of foreign assistance from the rich to the poor countries as a matter of right.[17] They saw nothing wrong in their own systems, and believed that they would, in fact, ensure them the highest development.

Because of superpower rivalry during the Cold War period there was no shortage of foreign assistance. Most of the loans were given on low interest terms. Foreign aid was easily available as long as the recipient country was ideologically sympathetic and supported the donor country on international issues.[18] Consequently, there was no incentive for the poor countries to modernize their economies.

Between 1970 and 1992, the external debt of poor countries grew by more than 2,000 percent and debt-service payment by 1,530 percent, thereby threatening the international financial system. Although a great deal of the debt was concentrated in Latin America, the debt problem of Africa was made more troublesome by declining per capita incomes and stagnant economies.[19]

Despite the debt crisis of the 1980s, international lending continued, once the borrowing country agreed to comply with the conditions of the International Monetary Fund (IMF). The IMF required reductions in government spending, growth of the money supply and wage increases in order to reduce imports, stimulate exports and make the country more self-sustaining.[20] In 1986, the IMF opened a structural adjustment policy (later known as the structural adjustment program) in order that loans could be given by international agencies, Western governments and commercial banks to countries that agreed to IMF conditions. This experience supplied a model to force economic development in the poor countries and transition economies (the former Soviet Union and Soviet bloc countries) during the Post-Cold War period.

When the Cold War ended the market economy and democracy had achieved triumph. Consequently, Western powers and international agencies began urging free markets, privatization of industry and agriculture, human rights and democracy, summed up as globalization, in exchange for foreign assistance. But, the Western powers and international agencies failed to grasp that the development imperatives they were proposing were incompatible with the centuries-old domestic system in poor countries. Therefore, despite the urging by the Western powers and international agencies, the old system in poor countries was still continuing through the new organizations.

For instance, ruling cliques in poor countries and transition economies complied with the privatization requests of Western powers and international agencies by selling "nationalized" industries to private monopolies (party-owned businesses and cronies) that were operating based on privileges similar to those of former state enterprises. They offered peasants so-called 99-year leases on land rather than property ownership. They conducted fig leaf elections and used parliament as a rubber stamp organization. In all these ways, the ruling cliques neutralized external pressure for development and continued to use foreign assistance to preserve their power and the domestic system. These leaders fear globalization because it will undermine their monopoly over resources and power by opening up the economy to domestic and external entrepreneurs.

ETHIOPIA'S FORMATION AND ECONOMIC DEVELOPMENT

Ethiopia is different from the rest of Africa in many ways. It is one of the oldest independent countries in the world. It had for centuries consisted of different ethnic groups and kingdoms, each with a history of its own, loosely held together by an imperial system. At the time of the second Industrial Revolution in the late nineteenth century, Ethiopia was an independent country. It was, however, undeveloped with no entrepreneurial group that could borrow and internalize modern technology. Ethiopia was able to see some of the inventions of the modern world as a result of foreign entrepreneurs who entered the country at this time. Serious economic development efforts began in Ethiopia only after the end of the Second World War.

Axum, Damot and Lasta

The ancient Kingdom of Axum, in present-day Tigrai, was the nucleus of Christian Ethiopia.[21] The rulers of Axum maintained themselves by controlling the trade routes of the African Red Sea coast. They supplemented their incomes with tributes and booty from the regions lying north and westward as far as the Nile Kingdom of Meroe in present-day Sudan. Their subjects lived off the land as agriculturists. They learned from the Yemenite settlers of the Habashat and Ge'ez groups how to use artificial irrigation, terracing and systems of canals.

Working on good terms with Greco-Egyptian merchants, Axum established commercial and maritime relations with the Byzantine Empire as early as the first century A.D. Trading establishments along the caravan routes and the coastal towns settled by Jews, Yemenites, Egyptians and Greeks flourished. Following in the footsteps of the commercial and maritime relations, Christianity entered Axum in the fourth century A.D.

During the first six centuries, Axum enjoyed a remarkable prosperity. The "degree of security, wealth, creative boldness and technical skill" of the Axumites can still be appreciated by the material relics of temples, towns, steles and obelisks, reservoirs and dams.

Map 1.1. Ethiopia (Based on Margery Perham, *The Government of Ethiopia*)
Gurage: 1. Soddo, 2. Ya Sabat bet, 3. Meskan, 4. Silte

The first rupture in the development of the Axumite Kingdom occurred in the eighth century A.D. as a result of the expansion of Islam from Arabia. The life of Axum was strangled when Arab traders and colonists destroyed the African Red Sea port of Adulis and occupied Massawa.

Islam provided a unifying structure and strength to nomadic tribes of Beja and Saho, living between the Sea and the plateau. The Islamized Zanafaj, a Beja group, became a powerful formation by controlling the sea routes and pillaging Axumite villages. They penetrated the Eritrean plateau by way of the valley of the Baraka. They overran much of the Hamasen. Most of the merchants in the coastal and trade route settlements left as central control weakened and the trade routes became dangerous and inaccessible. Consequently, the maritime commerce and revenue of Axum disappeared and its coinage became worthless. A number of kingdoms emerged over much of the territory that once belonged to Axum.[22]

In the succeeding centuries, the Axumites maintained their existence in the mountainous areas of Tigrai. They pursued austere development and Christian learning and spread into the inaccessible regions in the south and southwest (currently Begamder, Dambya, Gojjam, Agao-Meder, Damot and Amhara) occupied by the independent groups of Agao, who were Judaized and believers in indigenous religions.[23] The Agao groups maintained a national integrity as a result of the commercial and cultural currents of Judaism. The southward expansion of the Axumites encountered the powerful kingdom of Damot. Greater Damot controlled Simien in the north and the land of Agao, Gurage and Sidama, lying between Damot principality and the Gibe River.

In the tenth century, the powerful Queen of the Damot Kingdom, Yodit (Judith), nicknamed Esato (Fire) by the Christians, almost brought the embryonic Christian Kingdom to an end through devastating conquests until she was finally defeated and the Agao subjects Christianized by the Axumite settlers. The Agao accepted Christianity and blended it with their native tradition and Judaism to suit their heritage. After the defeat of Yodit, the Damot Kingdom was weakened and its influence limited.[24]

The Christian expansion brought about the end of the independent kingdoms of the Judaized Agao. The survivors, Bete Israel, called the Falasha by the Christians, still live in villages in the provinces of Dambya, Wogara and Armachoha. Most of them immigrated to Israel after the founding of the Jewish State. The Bete Israel are hardworking cultivators and artisans, who have not adopted commerce, the characteristic occupation of the Jewish dispersion. The Bete Israel are despised by the Christian community with whom they are forbidden to eat and whose house's they do not enter.

At the beginning of the first millennium, the royal power of the Christian Kingdom passed to the Zagwe family of Lasta, in present-day Wallo. Roha, the homeland of the Zagwe family, became the seat of the Christian Kingdom.

The period of the Zagwe Dynasty (1137–1270) was conducive to Christian expansion. Lalibela (1190–1225) was the most celebrated of the Zagwe rulers. He built the monolithic churches of Roha, which now bear his name. He used the influence of the Church to consolidate his Dynasty. Lalibela passed into tradition as a great saint.

Ifat, Sidama and Amhara (see Map 1.1)

During the Zagwe period, Ifat (in present-day Shawa) became the center of an Arab dynasty known as Makhzumi, founded in 896/7. Ifat proper was the plateau region of eastern Shawa, which included the slopes down to the valley of Awash (Hawash) River with a sphere of influence extending to the region around Zeila on the Gulf of Aden and the plain of Aussa.

In 1285, the Islamic formation was renewed by Ali ibn Wali Assma, who deposed the Makhzumite ruler and formed the new Walashma Kingdom of Ifat extending his rule over the Muslim States of Adal, Mora, Hobat and Jidaya.[25] The rulers of Ifat prospered through commerce and by controlling the trade routes, linking the interior with Zeila. They collected tributes from the less powerful Muslim kingdoms of Adal, Mora, Hobat and Jidaya. The Muslim population of Ifat lived by cultivating banana and sugar cane on their fertile land.

Islam, encouraging trade in articles and slaves, penetrated farther south to be embraced by the rulers of the Sidama states of Hadya, Fatajar, Dawaro and Bali, thereby ringing the massif of the Christian Kingdom of Ethiopia.[26]

The Muslim Sidama state of Hadya occupied the large territory between the Awash and Gibe Rivers. Its Muslim ruling class prospered through commerce. Hadya was renowned for supplying eunuchs to Arabia. Its subjects were a mixture of the Sidama, Gurage and the Chebo, who are descendants of the Gurage and Sidama.

The Gurage (the people of the country of Gur'a in Akkele Guzay, present-day Eritrea),[27] who are probably the descendants of Tigrayans and the Sidama, occupy the fertile, mountainous country south of the Awash, west of Lake Zway, north of Hadiya-Qabena and east of the Oromo River. The Gurage are mixed agriculturists and proficient traders and artisans well known for their hard work and entrepreneurial talent. The Gurage came in contact with the Christian Amhara, who mixed completely with them, influencing their language and religion. The Gurage include Christians, Muslims and believers in indigenous religions.[28] The town of Silte, lying at the foot of Mount Gurage, was the main Muslim commercial center. Another trading center of the Muslim Gurage was Amaya in Nonno territory.

In the 1870s, the Hadya were divided into two autonomous principalities: the northern half was called Qabena or Hadya Wambe and the southern principality, lying between the River Omo and the Tambaro, was called Hadya Tufta. Umar Baksa, a fortune seeker from Chaha Gurage, formed the state of Qabena. He became a Muslim to open commercial relations with the Muslim Kingdoms of Jimma and Limmu-Enarea; and consequently, he turned Qabena into an important commercial center, gathering around him merchants, soldiers of fortune, deserters and displaced people. He took the title of Imam and spread Islamic learning by making his subjects send their sons at age six or seven to schools in the mosques, where they were taught by masters to recite the whole of the Qur'an by heart.

The Muslim State of Tambaro formed the southern part of the large Hadya Kingdom. The Tambaro spoke the same language as their northern neighbors, the Christian Kambata. The agriculturist Alaba (Halaba) lived between Lake

Awassa and the Billate River, which separated them from the Kingdom of Wolayta. Their market center was Colito (Gulito) with a mosque of its own. In the fifteenth century, the Alaba were part of the Hadya Kingdom.

The State of Fatajar was situated on the western loop of the Awash River, occupying the extreme southeastern buttresses of Shawa. To the north of Fatajar was the Sultanate of Ifat. The three Muslim States of Ifat, Hadya and Fatajar occupied the strategic positions that provided footholds for further penetration of Islamic commerce and learning into the Christian Kingdom of Ethiopia.

The Muslim Sidama state of Dawaro (roughly in present-day Arsi) was situated south of Shawa, bordering on Ifat on the right bank of the Awash and extending southwards as far as the Wabi River. The Arsi were one of the Oromo pastoralist groups with some cultivators among them, living in permanent settlements. They occupied the region north of the Sidama region and south of the Karayu plain. They were organized under the gada or age-group system and did not form their own kingdom. Christian and Islamic settlements existed in the principal centers of the Arsi. In the second half of the nineteenth century, Islamic influence made headway under Sheik Nur Hussein, who also organized the Arsi resistance against the Shawa-Amhara expansion.

To the south of Dawaro was the State of Bale, stretching between the Wabi in the north and the Ganale Doria in the south, thereby including the Somali plain. The Sidama, who lived by cultivating their fertile land, largely inhabited the State of Bale. South of Bale, was Borana, home of the Oromo. The nomadic Borana are essentially cattle herders. They also keep some goats, sheep and camels. They live in simple villages of grass huts, built in places where they find water and grazing.

Between the tenth and twelfth centuries, Muslim establishments dotted the periphery of the Christian Kingdom of Ethiopia from Sawakin to east of Shawa on the fertile uplands of Ifat. The Muslim establishments that came between Ethiopia and the outside world played the essential role of economic intermediaries as long as they were on good turns with the Christian rulers. Muslim merchants controlled commercial activities in the Christian towns and became the trading partners of the Christian rulers, providing all royal trade connections with regional Muslim powers.

The commercial and cultural currents of Islam did not penetrate the Sidama Kingdoms of Enarea and Kafficho (see Map 1.1). These were the richest and strongest of the entire Sidama Kingdoms. They were situated in the area from which most of the gold, ivory, musk, incense, precious skins and slaves came. The Kingdom of Kafficho at one time extended from the fringe of the Sudanese lowlands in the west to the rift valley lakes in the east, and from the Omo River in the north to Lake Rudolf in the south.[29]

The prosperous kingldom of Kafficho was a hierarchically organized aristocratic society. At the peak was the Divine King, who was the high priest of the State Religion, owner of all land and supreme warlord. The summit of the State consisted of the Divine King and the Chiefs of the Seven Aristocratic Clans. The Chiefs had the power to limit the authority of the King and depose him. The land was divided into Crown land and hereditary fiefs, owned by free Kaffichos only. The Kafficho Kingdom had fiercely defended its independence against intruders until it was finally defeated and annexed by the Shawa Amhara at the end of the nineteenth century.[30]

Amhara

A new phase in the life of the Christian Kingdom began with the rise of Yekuno-Amlak, a local chief of Geshen and Ambasel, in Amhara (present-day Wallo). He took the royal power in a revolt against the reigning Zagwe Dynasty at the time when the Church split with the State over the position given to Roha by the Zagwe kings.

Yekuno-Amlak moved the center of the Christian Kingdom from Lasta to Tegulet in Shawa. In subsequent centuries, the Amhara rulers became the bulwark of Christian nationalism in Ethiopia along with the Axumite Church, engaging in life and death struggles against Islamic expansion over fertile territories and lucrative trade routes.[31]

The Amhara rulers contained Islamic pressure and extended their rule over the Muslim States. Amda-Syon (1314–44) turned Ifat, Hadya, Fatajar, Dawaro and Bale into tributary states. The Shawan regions of Manz (Manzeh) and Zega were entirely annexed and the boundaries of Ethiopia were carried to the edge of the plateau along the River Awash. Christianity acquired a new lease on life while Islamic influence in Sidamaland quickly faded away.

Yesehap (1414–29) acquired vast territory and resources by extending his empire to the north as far as Massawa and the Sudan plain, threatening the nomadic Tigre and Beja of the Sahil and upper Baraka. To the south the Empire consisted of the former Muslim Kingdoms and the many Sidama countries as far as and including Wolayta. The prosperous State of Enarea was seized with its rich gold mines and was brought in contact with Christianity for the first time. The Negus (King) Yesehaq occupied the port of Zeila on the east; consequently, he brought the Kingdom of Ifat to an end.

Yesehaq improved relations with Egypt; as a result, outside stimulus to development increased. Florentine craftsmen found their way to Ethiopia and soon took part in the building of Debrework in Gojjam. Turkish artisans settled in the country and initiated workshops for making coats of mail, swords and various other weapons. Egyptian Mamluks reformed Yesehaq's army and trained the soldiery in the use of Greek firearms. Egyptian Copts helped in reorganizing the system of tributes.

Zara-Yacob (1434–68) consolidated the conquests of his predecessors, building churches, endowing monasteries endowments and encouraging art and literature. He moved the royal center to Debre-Berhan, southeast of Tegulet. He divided up the provinces anew, created a new class of governors and fixed the tribute. During the reign of Zara-Yacob, urban centers appeared in the south of Shawa, at Entoto, in the neighborhood of Mount Menagesha, at Yarar, on the northern shores of Lake Zwai and in the slopes of Jibat.

Zara-Yacob overpowered the Muslim Sultanates and forced the Walashma rulers out of Ifat. The Muslim rulers subsequently established a new center at Dakar (a little southeast of present-day Harar) in Adal country, calling themselves kings of Adal. The Walashma removed themselves from the threat of the Amhara rulers, but were still within reach of the main trade route to the port of Zeila.

Adal (see Map 1.1)

In the sixteenth century, the prosperity of the Amhara rulers received an enormous setback as the expansion of the Ottoman Turks energized the Muslim Sultanates. At the same time, the Oromo expansion became an important variable in the equation of the Christian Empire.

In the early sixteenth century, Afari and Somali amirs replaced the Walashma leaders of the Adal Kingdom.[32] The royal power of the Adal Kingdom passed to Al-Jarad Abun ibn Adash with Zeila as his main center. He was then replaced by Sultan Abu Bakr ibn Muhammad, who transferred his headquarters from Dakar to Harar.

Imam Ahmad ibn Ibrahim Al-Ghazi, nicknamed Ahmad Grany (the left-handed) by the Amhara took over the Adal Kingdom from Sultan Abu Bakr after he built his power base in Hubat, the region between Gildessa and Harar. Once in complete control of the Adal Kingdom, Imam Ahmad began the conquest of the Christian Empire in 1529 by declaring jihad against the Christians and brought three-fourths of the Christian Empire under his control for fifteen years. Except for the monarchy and the Church, most of the Christian population submitted to the Imam and were Islamized en masse. Spoliations, burnings and massacre characterized the Great Conquest of Imam Ahmad. The accumulated wealth of the Amhara rulers and their subjects was looted. The political organization of Ethiopia was destroyed, along with towns, ancient buildings and many other valuable objects. Many Ethiopians were taken captive and sold into slavery. Peasants were pillaged and their fields went out of cultivation; consequently, severe famines broke out. Imam Ahmad made fortunes pursuing trade in gold, ivory, civet, incense, myrrh, drugs and slaves.

Soon came a turn of events in the region. The Portuguese penetration of the Arabian Sea trade reversed the prosperity of Imam Ahmad and the dominance of the Adalites in the region. The Portuguese raided the Arabian Sea areas and developed the trade route around the Cape of Good Hope to the Indies. Consequently, the Red Sea commerce and trading stations of Massawa, Zeila and Berbera declined.

In 1542 Imam Ahmad was defeated and killed at Weyna-Dega by the Portuguese and Ethiopia's Simien army under the leadership of Gelawdewos (1540–59). Gelawdewos readily recaptured most of the lost empire except the coastal establishments, controlled by Naibs or local representatives who lived by exacting dues and customs fees for their Turkish masters.

The successors of Imam Ahmad held out at Harar until the Amhara rulers wiped out the nobility and its military power by the 1570s. The center of the Adal Kingdom moved to Aussa under Imam Muhammed Jasa, a member of the Imam Ahmad family.

The Adalite State declined as a result of the Oromo and Afar raids. Its commercial revenue diminished as the Somali began to pillage the port of Zeila. In the 1670s, the royal power of Aussa passed into the hands of the Afar family and the once powerful Adalite dynasty with its Islamic threat to Christian Ethiopia disappeared forever. The Aussa Afar nobles, Asa Mara, held political power and economic authority over their subjects, Ado Mara. By the turn of the nineteenth century, Aussa became a tributary state of Ethiopia under Menelik.[33]

Harar (see Map 1.1).

In the 1640s, Harar broke away from the Aussa Sultanate under the leadership of Ali ibn Daud. In the succeeding centuries, Harar continued to serve as the chief center of Islamic learning.

Harar is an ancient city located in the foothills of the Amhar mountain. Its original inhabitants were the Islamized Adere. Harar had been an important center of commerce and Islamic learning for centuries. Harar was renowned for richly laden caravans, for its crowded and well-stocked markets and for the brilliance of its courts. Harari caravans traded with the rich provinces of southern Ethiopia, with Shawa and the Ogaden. From Harar caravans went to Zeila and Berbera.[34] The economic significance of Harar declined as a result of Oromo incursions until the Amir Nur, one of the successors of Imam Ahmad, negotiated a treaty with the Oromo and persuaded them to attend its markets and participate in its Islamic learning. The Oromo now make about half of the inhabitants of Harar. They belong to the Barentu, the second largest Oromo group. In the 1860s, the Oromo chiefs acquired wealth and rose to power; consequently, they were able to share state power in Harar with the Amir Muhammed ibn Ali. When Harar fell under the Egyptians (1875–85) the Oromo nobility lost its power. By the turn of the nineteenth century, Menelik of Shawa annexed Harar and thereby acquired a natural strongpoint for control of neighboring Oromo and Somali.[35] By the turn of the nineteenth century, Menelik of Shawa completed his annexation of the lands of the Somali Isa, Ogaden, Merrehan and Awilhan as far as the Juba and Wabi Shebeli. His conquest ignited a national resistance by a Somali wadad (priest) Muhammad ibn Abdallah of the Dulbahanta group, who declared his jihad against Ethiopia and the British.[36]

Muhammad Abdullah acquired religious prestige and leadership by making pilgrimages to Mecca where he joined the tariqa (teachings) of Muhammad Salih. He claimed the position of Khalifa of Silihiyya with the authority to preach Islam, teach its ritual and initiate new members. He called all Somalis to a disciplinary religious life in accordance with the precepts of Islam. He gave the name Darawish to his followers, who came from different Somali groups. The corps of his force was called the Hajatu. He declared an open rebellion against the British in 1899, but lost to their army. He died in 1920 after the final British expedition against the Somali resistance.

Gondar

By the beginning of the seventeenth century, Christian Ethiopia had lost the territories south of Shawa to the Oromo expansion. The Empire was cut back to the natural boundaries of the Abai (Blue Nile) and Awash Rivers with Oromo groups occupying the regions east of the plateau.

The biggest achievement of Christian Ethiopia in the seventeenth century was the establishment of Gondar by Atse Fasil (1667–82). Atse Fasil courted the neighboring Islamic powers to save Ethiopia from Portuguese penetration. Fasil therefore broke all contacts with the West. Ethiopia was isolated for a long period of time.

Agriculture prospered in Christian Ethiopia during this time and the commercial significance of Gondar was considerable. Gondar provided a market for local and imported goods. The importance of the Sennar trade route increased and adjacent trading centers, such as Emfras on the coast of Lake Tana, rapidly developed. Since the Christian rulers of Gondar were on good terms with the neighboring Muslim powers, commerce and the prosperity of Muslim merchants in the country increased.

Alarmed by the advancement of Muslim Ethiopians and productive minorities, Yohannes I (1667–82), son of Fasil, passed a discriminatory law, ordering the Muslims and Bete Israel in Gondar to live in a separate quarter on the banks of the Qaha River. The Franks, descendants of the Portuguese, were ordered to leave the country unless they joined the national Orthodox Church. The Muslims were not allowed to own land and engage in agriculture; consequently, they became much more proficient in commerce and crafts, thereby dominating the trade of the region. Furthermore, their social oppression brought them closer to the subjected groups of Bete Israel, Sidama, Oromo and Bani Shangul. Many Oromo groups accepted Islam as a social defense against the Christian nationalism.[37]

Iyasu The Great (1682–1706) instituted social and economic reforms, something rare in the history of Christian Ethiopia. The Feteha Negest (Civil Code) was revised and the laws of the land were reformed. Uniform customs rates were established to check the rapacity of collectors of customs duties and to promote trade.

Iyasu tried to take Ethiopia out of isolation. External trade relations with Cairo and Europe improved with the help of Levantine merchants, who for centuries handled transit trade for Ethiopia. The peaceful relation with the Funj Sultanate that controlled the Nile Valley in the Sudan and the control over the Arab nomads by the Funj assured the security of the caravans between Gondar and Cairo.[38]

Oromo

In the first half of the sixteenth century the Oromo pastoralists, the Illm Oromo or sons of Oromo, their eponymous ancestor began to emigrate en masse to find new ranges. One group came from the southwest along the corridor between Mount Walabu and Lake Abaya, and another from the south ascending the Juba and Wabi river valleys.[39] The Oromo raided and overran vast areas of land. The Dawe sub-group of the Borana occupied the State of Bale under the gada Melbah attracted by its rich pastures and water while succeeding gadas[40] invaded the States of Dawaro and Fatajar. From Bale, they turned against the Harar Sultanate.

Having reached the Awash River, some of the Oromo groups penetrated into the northwest while others moved northeast following the rich valley of the Awash; consequently, they occupied the fertile regions in the east of the plateau by the beginning of the seventeenth century. The cycles of gadas that began with the gada Harmufu or Dulu penetrated the provinces of Gan and Angot even into Amhara and Begamder, the heart of the Ethiopian empire. The other Oromo groups, consisting of the Gimbichu, Ada and Mecha groups probably migrated from between Mount Walabu and Lake Abaya and travelled towards the sources of the Gibe River. They made Wallega their new homeland and Walab their sacred mountain, from which the Mecha group invaded the Sidama States. They spread into the southwest as far as the prosperous states of Enarea and Kafficho and split the latter into two parts: present-day Kafficho and Anfillu—north of the Sobat River.[41]

Afan-Oromo or the Oromo language is one of the most widely spoken languages in Ethiopia today. It is divided into two major dialects: (1) The northern dialects of (a) Mecha, spoken by the Limmu, Guma, Goma, Jimma, Gera, Leka, Lakamt, and Nonno. (b) Tulama, spoken throughout Shawa and (c) Borana, spoken by the Borana, Jamjam, Arsi, Ittu, Karayu and the Warra Daya of Somaliland; and (2) the southern dialects, spoken by the Bararetta and Kofira Oromo, who live on the banks of the Tana River in Kenya.[42]

The Somali (see Map 1.1)

The Somali pastoralists also accomplished a successful movement at the time of the Oromo expansion. Their movement started in the fourteenth century when the Hawiya or Ajuran migrated to the region between the lower courses of the Wabi and Juba rivers. The Somali spread westward out of their limited and arid region and occupied all the steppes of the Ogaden and the first foothills of the central massif as far as Harar. In the south, they occupied the Banadir and the valleys of the Wabi Shebeli and Juba, from which they pushed the Oromo northwest towards the valleys of the upper tributaries of the Juba, where the Borana now live. During the process of pastoral expansion, some of the Somali mixed with the Oromo. The descendants of this fusion are the Rahanwen, Dijil Somali mixed with Oromo.

The majority of the Somali were nomadic herdsmen, living a communal life in the forest and steppe regions. Town dwellers and agriculturists made up a small portion of the Somali, living in settlements and villages along the rivers. The town dwellers played an important economic role. Representatives of the nomads travelled to the towns regularly to exchange their sheep, goats and other produce, such as hides, milk and butter for rice, dates and textiles. The mosques and coffeehouses served as the community center of townsmen for conducting all their affairs from marriages to business transactions.

The Oromo Kingdoms of the Gibe or the Southwest (see Map 1.1)

The Mecha Oromo, who spread towards the sources of the Gibe River, formed, in the early nineteenth century, the highly organized despotic monarchies between the Omo and the Didessa Rivers. The best known were Limmu-Enarea, Guma, Goma, Jimma-Kakka and Gera.[43] The Oromo and Sidama kings, in contrast to the Amhara rulers, did not have a paternal sense of responsibility for their subjects. They sold their subjects into slavery as a punishment for minor offences and for non-payment of taxes. Occasionally, children were taken from their parents by the rulers in lieu of unpaid taxes. In years of famine, the poor Oromo and Sidama sold their own children when they were unable to feed them. The Christian population was prohibited from engaging in slave trade by ecclesiastical and civil law, but the buying and keeping of personal slaves were not forbidden. Despite the prohibition, many Christians were sold in secrecy by the Christians themselves or kidnapped by passing caravans.[44]

The Oromo rulers acquired prosperity and power by taking over the Sidama States and developing commerce, working on good terms with Muslim merchants coming from Warjihe in Shawa, Darita Maryam in Begamder and from the Egyptian Sudan. The Oromo rulers warmly welcomed these merchants to handle transit trade in coffee, hides, precious skins, ivory, gold and slaves, thereby assuring their own prosperity and power. In the mid-nineteenth century, the Oromo rulers embraced Islam through the agency of the Muslim merchants and their subjects followed suit. The Gibe Kingdoms were all agricultural economies and used slave labor. The continuous warfare between the Sidama and Oromo produced captives who were enslaved for profit.

The Goma Kingdom with its capital at Hagaro was situated at the center of the Gibe Oromo formations. Its ruling family was the Awallini. The Goma Oromo were known for their hard work and intelligence. Their fertile land produced teff, corn, coffee and cotton. In 1886, Menelik of Shawa incorporated Goma into the Ethiopian Empire.

Limu-Enarea was established by Bofo, a renowned war leader and son of Aba Boku. Its capital was Sakka. Limu-Enarea was also annexed by Menelik in 1891. The hilly region of Guma belonged to the royal family of the Adami. Its king was Jawe Oncho. The Shawans under Menelik annexed Guma in 1885. The State of Gera, rich in pastures and forests, produced coffee. Its former capital was Chala or Cira. Gera enjoyed a period of prosperity under its king, Abba Magal. Gera was brought into the Ethiopia Empire in 1887.

The Kingdom of Jimma was founded by Abba Gomol on the old Sidama Kingdom of Bosha. It covered the valley of the Gibe and was confined within the area formed by the course of the Omo to the east and south, by Mount Botor in the northeast, and the mountains of Limu and Goma to the north and west. Hirmata was the great market center of the Jimma Kingdom. Jimma was a well-populated, fertile plateau country, producing corn, vegetables and coffee. Abba Jifar, son of Abba Gomol, submitted peacefully to Menelik of Shawa in 1883; consequently, he was allowed local autonomy that was retained until the 1930s.

Abba Jifar developed Jimma into a leading commercial center in the southwest by decreasing taxes and customs dues. He wanted Jimma to be a center of Islamic studies and therefore became a strict Muslim himself encouraging the fuqara (thinkers) to settle and teach in Jimma.

Abba Jifar divided his country into seventy koros (districts) according to the Sidama system and each district was administered by an Abba Koro. His country consisted of residents from Shawa, Gojjam and Wallo. He recruited his bodyguards from the Wallo settlers. Attracted by the lucrative trade in Jimma, Yemeni traders settled in Jimma and intermarried with the natives. Their descendants formed the merchant class in Jimma.

The Western Oromo Monarchies (see Map 1.1)

The Oromo Monarchies of the west consisted of Gudru, Jote Abba Iggu's Leka Kellem, Leka Lakemti (Nakemti), Leka Sayo and Nonno. They all prospered through agriculture and trade. Gama-Moras formed his Gudru State by accumulating wealth from trade in the Assandabo market, where he collected toll assisted by his own troops.[45] During the Shawan expansion in the late nineteenth century, the western Oromo States submitted without resistance in return for internal autonomy. This lasted until the 1930s when they were brought under the direct control of the Imperial Government.

The Highland or Northern Oromo (Wallo, Yeju and Raya) Ascendancy

The northern Oromo (see Map 1.1), unlike the other Oromo groups, came in close contact with the highland Amhara. They intermarried with them, became bilingual, and adopted settled agricultural life along with the social and political institutions of the Amhara. They maintained their Oromo identity by embracing Islam. The most northern of the highland Oromo are the Raya, called Azebo by the Tigrayans from the name of the country they occupy— the great plain east of the plateau, watered by the Ala and Golima rivers. They are primarily pastoralists. In their past, they lived off raiding the caravan routes between Tigrai and Shawa. Those who lived in the villages, such as, Corebetta were settled cultivators. The Raya speak Oromo and Tigrinya as a result of Tigrayans, who settled among them.[46]

The Yeju Oromo occupy the semi-tropical fertile country south of the Raya and north of Wallo, bordered by the Aussa on the east, Amhara on the West and Lasta on the north. The center of Yeju is Waldia, followed by the towns of Mokareet and Merta. The people of Yeju were known for their self-sufficient economy. They grew their own grains, cotton, oil seeds and cattle; and consequently, avoided the sufferings of starvation and famine. They had their own potters, tanners and smiths. The Yeju Oromo had intermarried with their eastern neighbors, the Afar-Saho. Yeju produced rich and famous families, such as, the Warra Shaikh, descendants of the legendary Umar Shaikh, who came from across the Red Sea. Ras Gugsa and Ras Ali belonged to the Warra Shaikh family and ruled Ethiopia in cohesion with the Wallo chiefs from 1756 up to 1853.[47]

The country of the Wallo Oromo is separated from the Amhara country by the Bachilo, from Gojjam by Abai (the Blue Nile), from Shawa by the Wanchit and Jama, in the northeast by the Mille and the east by the Danakil plain. Most of Wallo is Amhara country, especially the highest regions of the plateau in the east and south, the Amhara-Saynt region west of Dessie, the massifs of Legambo and Legaida and the Warra Illu plateau.

The Wallo Oromo consist of seven sub-groups, called Sabat Wallo Bet, the Seven Wallo Houses, by the Amhara. The Warra Himano speak more Amharinya than Afan-Oromo, The Warra Babo and the Warra Kallu speak Afan-Oromo and the others Amharinya mixed with Afan-Oromo. The sub-groups near Aussa speak Afan-Oromo mixed with Dankali (Afari).

The Wallo Oromo are cultivators and poor compared to their Yeju neighbors. They are much engaged in saying their wodacha (Islamic prayer and blessing) on Wednesdays and Fridays till midday. They believe that they receive revelations from Allah (God) during the ceremony. They assemble early morning, say their prayers, take coffee or tea and smoke tobacco. They ask Allah to give them cows, clothes and whatever they need, and to give their chiefs gold and silver.[48]

The main centers of the Wallo Oromo are Dessie, Warra Illu, Akasta and Batie. They produced ruling families, which claimed Arab descent. Imam Muhammed Ali (Negus Mikael, King Mikael—after he became a Christian) came from one of these leading families. The Wallo nobility became powerful during the reign of Iyoas (1756–69) whose mother was a Wallo princess. The Wallo Oromo formed the royal guards and the relatives of Iyoas became governors and enriched themselves. Thus, from 1756 up to 1853, the Yeju and Wallo nobility maintained cohesion and ruled Christian Ethiopia in Gondar. Ras Ali I of the Warra Shaikh family controlled the imperial power in 1788 and founded the Oromo Dynasty that ruled the Ethiopian Empire for many years. Gugsa Marsa of the Warra Shaikh, for instance, ruled Ethiopia from 1799 up to 1825.[49]

Gugsa Marsa rose to prominence gradually dispossessing the Tigrai/Amhara nobility. He issued a proclamation that had an element of land reform; and consequently, earned the support of the peasantry. He declared a state ownership of all lands because he said that the land belonged to Rabbi (God) and had no owner on earth other than the state. He proclaimed, "The land belongs to Rabbi; man can be no more than the usufructuary. He renders it fertile by his efforts and passes away; the earth swallows him up and flourishes still. What is a landowner whose property is stronger than himself? Holders of lordly estates and holders of fiefs, let me say to you that there is no hereditary right of suzerainty. Rabbi gives it to whom he pleases; he has given it to me, Gugsa! I am the lord of the land; you are beholden to me for all of it, and I alone allocate it at my pleasure."[50] Allocate, he did. He converted the fiefs of the Tigrai/Amhara nobility into temporary fiefs, which he then granted to his officials and followers.

In the early twentieth century, the Wallo Oromo nobility once again took control of Ethiopia during the reign of Lijj Iyasu (1909–17). Lijj Iyasu was born to Negus Mikael (Imam Muhammad Ali) of the Warra Himenu chiefly family and Woizero Shawa-Aregash, the daughter of Menelik of Shawa. Lijj Iyasu began reviving Islam to counter the dominance of the Christian Shawan nobility. He also started courting the Central Powers. He believed that the defeat of the Allies might allow Ethiopia to push Italy out of Eritrea and Somalia. Thus he sought an alliance with Imam Seyyid Muhammad Abdullah, who had long pursued an anti-colonialist war against the British and Ethiopia. He replaced the old guard of governors with his own. He also tried to integrate Muslims into the administration. His important task was nation building, not imperial exploitation. His method, however, threatened the Christian Shawan nobility, among them Dejazmach Teferi Makonnen (later Haile Selassie I).

The Shawan nobility viewed Lijj Iyasu's efforts to include Muslims into the administration with extreme disdain. He believed, however, his policy would reduce the Empire's chronic unrest and benefit the economy. The Shawan nobility believed that his policy of seeking alliance with Imam Seyyid Muhammad Abdullah was treasonous. His enemies thought that his continued leadership would plunge Ethiopia into war with the Allies and also lead to civil strife. Feeling alienated, the Shawan nobility marched on Addis Ababa and replaced him by Zawditu (Empress Zawditu), Menelik's daughter, in 1917, with Ras Tafari Makonnen as regent and heir to the throne.[51]

Regionalist Struggles and Imperial Reunification

The Yeju-Wallo Oromo dominance at Gondar from 1756 up to 1853 undermined the interest of the Tigrai/Amhara nobility. As a result, the alienated Tigrai/Amhara nobility, assisted by the Church that had been always foremost in fomenting revolts against the Oromo, engaged in regionalist struggles. By the early 1840s, the imperial system virtually collapsed and four entirely independent States emerged out of the debris of the Christian Empire of Ethiopia: Sahle Selassie's Shawa, Wube's Simien, Tigrai and Lasta, Goshu's Gojjam, and Negus Mikael's various Amhara provinces (Damot, Begamder, Dembya and the capital Gondar).

Each State conducted a separate development with its own army as a sovereign power, engaging in treaty making with the West. The only common bond among these States was the Church, whose power had already diminished. The Kingdom of Shawa, largely cut off from the rest of the country by the Wallo Oromo, was able to make a considerable advance by expanding its frontiers under a series of kings.[52] Tewodros of Qwara conquered the regional sovereigns and unified the divided Empire.with a new center at Magdala in Amhara country. Emperor Tewodros ruled Ethiopia from 1855 up to 1868.

Tewodros became wealthy and powerful by raiding the trade routes between Ethiopia and the Sudan. He acquired military skills by engaging in border defense against Egyptian intruders. He inherited from his uncle Kinfu the chieftain of the frontier province of Qwara. His large personal following and his education, received in the Tana Monastery, were advantages over his fellow chiefs. He built a powerful army loyal to him. He also instituted administrative and social reforms.

Emperor Tewodros divided the regions into small units and appointed his own trusted governors, thereby formed a new nobility. He confiscated some of the Church lands in order to maintain his administration and numerous soldiers. The clerics later turned out to be his greatest enemies. He was a social reformer in his own right and "wished to reform the feudal system, to have paid governors and judges and to disarm the people."[53] He used Christianity as a unifying ideology, but his unification policy drew opposition from Non-Christians. Tewodros fought an unending battle to enforce his reforms; consequently, he degenerated into a cruel tyrant.

Tigrayan Ascendancy

After Tewodros, the imperial power was taken by Yohannes, a Tembien Chief in Tigrai. During the reign of Emperor Yohannes, the European scramble for Africa was at its peak; as a result, Ethiopia was distracted by external intruders. The opening of the Suez Canal energized the colonial ambitions of Western powers. Muhammad Ali of Egypt (under Turkish influence) was raiding Ethiopian territory to extend his conquest to the Ethiopian source of the Blue Nile, from which Egypt receives its great supplies of water. The Mahdist movement in eastern Sudan also awakened the Islamic threat to Christian Ethiopia.[54]

Despite external intrusions, Emperor Yohannes made some efforts to continue with the development of the Christian Empire. He controlled Keren and secured the use of the Massawa Port. In the south Menelik of Shawa extended the empire over the Sidama-Oromo lands and secured essential trade routes. Yohannes endowed the Church and encouraged the clerics to spread Christianity as a unifying ideology. He ordered Muslims to build churches in their localities and pay tithes to their parish priests. Muslim officials of the Government were required to accept baptism or resign their posts. Priority to own land was given to Christians. Thus, wealthy Muslim traders became Christians just to buy land in Adwa, Hamasen and Akkele Guzay. His religious unification policy further alienated the Muslim population of Ethiopia.[55]

Eritrea

In 1980 Italian colonialists through treaties and military intrusions of the Red Sea coast carved out their colony of Eritrea. Historically, the Christian society of the central Eritrean plateau was an offshoot of the Tigrayan formation in Ethiopia proper. Each enda or kinship group was organized into restenyatat (landowners) and makhelai-alet (people amidst, who held land as sedbi (tenants) or by right of purchase called worqi. Only members of the restenyatat family were elected to the office of cheqa-shum (village chief) and shumonya or meslane (district chief). Top leadership positions belonged to powerful local families who ran the military and civilian administration, collected taxes and represented Ethiopian emperors in the Bahre-Medr, the maritime province.

The Bilen and Tigre-speaking groups of Eritrea (the tribal federations of Bilen, Marya, Mansa, Bait Asgede and Beni Amer) were divided into a ruling caste and a serf caste. The Bait Asgede were the rulers and lived off the Tigre serfs. The Tigre serfs received protection and the right to use the land and livestock of their masters in return for supplying them with grain, milk and butter. They helped their masters with paying off blood money and gave animals as gifts at weddings or death of nobles.

Muslims in Hamassen, Akele Guzay and Serai were denied resti (ancestral land) by imperial decree whereas it was the hereditary right of a Christian family within the enda. Muslims lived off trade and as tenants.

The Italian colonialism did not alter the traditional order much. Noble-serf relationships were still strong. The Italians invested their favorite chiefs with more resti. In places like Keren and Agordat they carried out cosmetic changes reducing the more onerous obligations.

The Italians used Eritrea for a military base for further colonial intrusion and as an outlet for export of raw materials to Italy. They deliberately neglected both agriculture and industry. In order to stimulate recruiting, they denied agricultural concessions to Italian colonists. Consequently, they did not have to alienate native land except from the rebellious chiefs. Italian agriculture in Eritrea was limited apart from such areas as Pendici on the eastern slopes of the altipiano and Tessenie and a few experimental farms. Some of the best agricultural lands around Agordat and Tessenie were left unfarmed.

Italian colonists worked in garages, engineering shops or small businesses that catered to military needs. Eritreans outside their community served as employees of Italian businesses and households. They worked as porters and stevedores. They were office messengers and soldiers in the colonial administration.

The campaign against Ethiopia in 1935 led to a large inflow of Italians to Eritrea. Business activities increased due to the campaign requirements and the consumption needs of the colonial population. In 1941 the military needs of the Allied and American projects further stimulated the economy. Agriculture and industry were energized. Eritreans opened their own businesses. They worked as restaurateurs, shop owners, mechanics, machine-minders and machine operators, masons, bricklayers, fitters, clerks, teachers and medical technicians. Political activists opposed to the colonial rule came out of these new social groups. They formed their own political parties during the British Military Administration of Eritrea in 1941–1952.

When Ethiopia became independent in 1941, many Eritreans came to Ethiopia to fill positions in various professional and technical areas or start their own businesses. Many more came after the federation of the two countries in 1952 to work in the government, open businesses and pursue modern education. Most of them became quite successful and their success was not viewed as a threat by the society. But in 1962 the federal system was abolished and Eritrea was brought under the direct control of the central government. This ignited rebellion and renewed the old problem of regionalism.

Shawan Ascendancy and Modernization Phase I

Ethiopia saw unprecedented unification, imperial expansion and modernizing attempts in the late nineteenth and early twentieth centuries during the reign of Emperor Menelik (1889–1913). His famous reign first as King of Shawa and later as Emperor of Ethiopia coincided with the European scramble for Africa, the first phase of the colonial period and the Second Industrial Revolution. Menelik opened up his country to the West and was able to accumulate more wealth and power than his predecessors had ever known. He initiated modernization and accomplished the most successful imperial unification that Ethiopia had ever seen.

The principal change in agriculture was the introduction of commercial farming for the first time into the country by foreign entrepreneurs. Commercial cultivation of coffee began in the early twentieth century in Harar and other places. The opening of the inland port of Gambela on the Baro River increased the export of coffee to the Sudan. The construction of the Addis Ababa-Djibouti railway facilitated the rapid growth of the coffee plantations in Harar. Foreign entrepreneurs established cotton, rubber and fiber plantations. Modern cattle farms were started during the same period, enabling the country to export live animals by rail to Djibouti.

The opening of Anglo-Ethiopian relations in 1897 brought many Indian merchants to Ethiopia which helped the expansion of commerce. Other nationalities, such as, Arabs, Armenians, French, Greeks and Jews also played a prominent role in the development of domestic and external trade. By the late nineteenth century, external trade in coffee, provided by the farms around Harar and the forests of the southern provinces, had already begun. Ethiopia's principal exports at this time comprised ivory, gold, coffee, salt, civet, wax, hides and skins, oilseeds, grains and live animals. Ethiopia's imports consisted of textiles and cotton goods, firearms, consumer goods, and petroleum products among others.[56]

Ethiopia witnessed the emergence of modern cities comprising a considerable number of merchants and artisans. The most important modern city, established by Emperor Menelik himself in the 1880s, was Addis Ababa (New Flower), which played a significant role in the emergence of a market economy. Menelik controlled the distribution of land for the new city and in the surrounding rural areas that supplied agricultural produce to Addis Ababa.

The establishment of Addis Ababa and the number of innovations that followed attracted many foreign entrepreneurs and artisans to come to Ethiopia. A number of Indian and Arab craftsmen were engaged in building activities. There were a large number of Armenian small traders and artisans, and Italians who worked as masons. A number of Greeks were engaged in house building operations; some of them established shops, flour mills, brick and liquor factories, oil presses and bakeries. Attracted by the employment opportunities of Addis Ababa, a large number of peasants, especially, migrant workers from Gurage came from the central provinces. The Soddo Gurage made up the largest segment of the labor force in Addis Ababa at this time, working as artisans, small traders, farm hands, laborers and domestic service providers.

The nucleus of the emerging city of Addis Ababa was Menelik's palace. Court and diplomatic affairs were concentrated at the palace as well as the affairs of agriculture and industrial enterprises. The requirements of the Emperor and his large entourage provided the market for the establishment of commercial enterprises in and around the compound. The agricultural and industrial enterprises of the palace employed six to eight thousand people.

In the early twentieth century, the City of Dire Dawa was established. Dire Dawa flourished rapidly as a result of its advantageous location on the Addis Ababa-Djibouti railway line. It took over the caravan routes of the south from the famous, old trading center of Harar.

Addis Ababa

The Emperor introduced a modern financial institution and issued a new currency. A banking monopoly was granted by the Emperor's concession to the National Bank of Egypt—behind which was a European banking group. A major monetary revolution came in the late nineteenth century through the issuance of the first Ethiopian modern currency, although the Maria Theresa dollar still continued to circulate.

Trade was enhanced by the advances made in the sphere of transport and communications during this time. The first such advances were the establishment of shipping service on the Baro River, the construction of roads and bridges and the famous Addis Ababa-Djibouti railway. Along with these came the establishment of postal, telephone and telegram services. Electric light and telephone services first reached Menelik's Palace in 1903. The coming of the printing press and newspapers in the late nineteenth century inaugurated a modern era of disseminating information in Ethiopia. Menelik encouraged modern education and medicine. Various missionary societies were instrumental in the introduction of modern education and medicines at this time.

The Empire was vastly extended and essential trade routes were acquired through Shawan military conquest. At the same time, various regions and communities that had never been within the reach of the Imperial Government were brought under the Ethiopian Empire for the first time. The

Shawans, not yet wedded to the wage system, introduced in the conquered territories an onerous gult (fief) system to maintain themselves. On the positive side of the balance sheet, they introduced bureaucracy, the Christian religion and learning, the plough and the cultivation of the teff staple.

Menelik initiated modernizing attempts by opening up his country to the West, however, life in many parts of the country remained the same as it had been in the previous centuries. Menelik put very little of his fortune to commercial and technical uses. Practically the whole of his funds went for building his own army.[57]

Shawan Continuity and Haile Selassie's First Reign

Emperor Haile Selassie attempted to continue with the modernizing attempts of Menelik in his first reign from 1928 up to 1935. Harar was his power base, which he inherited from his famous father Ras Makonnen. He strengthened his wealth and influence by obtaining the concession of Wallo as his fief and establishing strong contacts with the West. In 1929, he became Emperor of Ethiopia in a revolt and began to build a unitary state loyal to him. In 1931, he granted a constitution, the first in the history of the land, and instituted a parliament with two chambers for the main purpose of bringing the feudal chiefs under his direct control in Addis Ababa. The Constitution gave no hint of an official religion; consequently, Muslim Ethiopians were allowed religious liberty for the first time. They acquired land freely, developed commercial activities and held important government positions, especially in regions where Islam was predominant and official recognition was given to important Islamic holidays.

Haile Selassie relied on the West to modernize his country. But no significant changes occurred during his first reign. He sold the salt monopoly and some road and mining concessions that paid him modest royalties. He looked for foreign capital to build a dam at Abai (the Blue Nile). This did not materialize because of the Great Depression.

Italian Occupation

Haile Selassie's first reign was interrupted by the Italian occupation in 1936, which lasted five years (1936–41). After they occupied Ethiopia, the Italians began to create a colonial empire of Italian East Africa consisting of what they called Amhara, Shawa, Galla-Sidamo, Harar, Eritrea and Italian Somaliland, which included the Ogaden.

Italian colonialism was short-lived, but brought a dramatic impact in such areas as infrastructure and external trade. The Italians allocated 133 million

British pounds for the first phase of their colonial development, an amount far greater than the British allocated for their African colonies.[58]

In record time, the Italians built a network of roads (4,410 miles) and bridges, bearing the mark of their engineering at its best. The huge investment in road works rapidly paid off as transportation cost fell from 60 cents to 8 cents a ton on paved roads and to 16 cents on other roads.[59]

The colonial impact on Ethiopia's external trade was also significant. Almost all the requirements for the development of Ethiopia and the consumption needs of a large member of Italian colonists had to be imported from Italy. Ethiopia's exports had to go to Italy to finance the imports. Ethiopia's imports increased astronomically while its exports fell. Most of Ethiopia's traditional export items were not being exported. The foreign merchants with experience in Ethiopia's import-export trade were expelled and replaced by Italian merchants. The Italians divided the country by ethnic group and religion, and favored Muslims over Christians to undermine the domestic merchants, especially the Soddo Gurage.

Imperial Restoration and Modernization Phase II

Liberation came to Ethiopia in 1941 when the Second World War was at its peak. As a result of a 1942 treaty with Britain, Ethiopia began to receive British subsidies and advisors. A loan of 2.5 million British pounds, something new in the history of Ethiopia, was made available in return for free use of immovable property of Ethiopia required by the British forces during the war. Owing to the war conditions, Ethiopia's external trade began to revive. Most of the foreign merchants, who were expelled by the Italians came back.

Upon the end of the Second World War, the Emperor allied with the United States of America for assistance. A new currency was issued and Ethiopia became a member of the International Monetary Fund (IMF). New laws were passed and the bureaucracy was modernized. The Government played an active role in shaping the direction of economic development, but the economy remained free-market-oriented. Infrastructure was built and investment was made in urban development. The Parliament was restored although it remained a rubberstamp organization. There were, however, fair and free elections for the House, conducted periodically throughout the country without incidents. The Parliament represented the beginning of a democratic experience and a revolution in social ideas in a country where noble birth had been the only qualification for governing. However, Haile Selassie did not liberalize the political process. He also failed to turn land over to the peasantry.

Haile Selassie, the Education Emperor, strongly believed in expanding modern education for Ethiopia's development but was little interested in political and land reforms. He introduced free public and university education for all. In 1961 he established the first university in the country, Haile Selassie I University, and gave one of his palaces for that purpose. His commitment to modern education was unmatched by any leader in the history of Ethiopia.

Ethiopia's increased contact with the West during this period created more opportunities for trade and development. Ethiopia's trade volume doubled between 1964 and 1974. Coffee accounted for 60 percent of Ethiopia's export earnings, and the United States of America alone bought 70 percent of Ethiopia's coffee. The United States supplied most of the foreign aid and technical assistance.

Private sector investment was encouraged. The government, however, was the major partner with foreign investors. Domestic entrepreneurs were involved in a wide range of activities, such as manufacturing, import-export and distribution, restaurants, hotels, banking, insurance and agribusiness. In the 1960s and early 1970s contract farming by private entrepreneurs began to modernize the countryside, and the economy showed promising growth rates. However, Ethiopia was still predominantly a subsistence economy living under the constant threat of famine. In 1973/74, Ethiopia was hit by the worst famines in years on top of a worldwide economic crisis. By September 1974, Emperor Haile Selassie was overthrown by the armed forces that had given him a solid base of power for 30 years.

Military Government

The Military Regime of Mengistu Hailemariam dissolved Parliament and established a Marxist-Leninist, one-party State. A command growth model was adopted for the development of Ethiopia. Consequently, land and all major industrial and trading activities were owned by the state. All foreign managers and entrepreneurs left the country because of the Government's "nationalization" policy. The Government confiscated commercial farms and launched a radical program of rural collectivization. Domestic entrepreneurs were discriminated against and persecuted.[60]

The nationalization of land by the Government abolished rent payments to landlords. This boosted peasant income temporarily, but the income increment was wiped out by population growth. Food production per capita declined, and food imports increased. The production and export of industrial crops, such as, coffee, oil seeds, and pulses declined. The periodic volatility of coffee prices reduced foreign exchange earnings. The government formed a coffee-marketing corporation and took over the coffee trade completely. The Coffee Marketing Corporation bought all high quality coffee for export, leaving only the portion that had not met export standards for domestic consumption. A significant portion of the domestic demand went unmet. Coffee smuggling to non-coffee growing regions and abroad became common.

About 95 percent of the coffee was still produced by peasant cultivators. There was a shortage of seasonal labor for coffee picking because the hiring of labor and free movement of peasants were prohibited. The government relaxed its collectivization pressure in the coffee- producing regions by mid-1988. There were shortages of basic food and consumer goods. Prices were extremely high because domestic production was limited or non-existent to fill the gap created by import restrictions. Interregional grain trade was restricted, which impaired the national grain market by depressing prices in surplus areas while inflating them in shortage areas. The price control policy was hurting the majority of the population by creating shortages and underground markets.

Private entrepreneurs could not buy land, invest in agriculture or accumulate wealth under the socialist system. The under-capitalization of agriculture worsened. The government introduced a progressive agriculture income tax, thereby creating a disincentive for investment in agricultural improvement. Because the gainful use of land and other property was not legal, it became very difficult to attract private investment despite a 1988 policy permitting private investment in agriculture and other activities.

Peasant producers made compulsory deliveries of grains to the Agricultural Marketing Corporation at a fixed price. They sold the rest to grain traders at a free market price. The main goal of the Corporation was to provide grains to urban dwellers at low prices. The Corporation fixed its own buying price and this depressed agricultural production by holding the price below market. Most of the Corporation's purchases were undertaken in the major grain surplus regions of Gojjam, Shawa and Arsi. Grain traders were required to sell all purchases from Gojjam and Arsi and 50 percent of their other purchases to the Corporation at what was called the wholesale buying price. Peasants and grain traders were not allowed to transport food grains out of any of these regions until the policy was relaxed in 1988 as a result of pressure from the World Bank.

The Agricultural Marketing Corporation sold food grains through its own retail stores in the urban centers. These stores often had short supplies; consequently urban dwellers were forced to buy from grain traders at a higher price.

Foreign trade was a state monopoly. Foreign currency was rationed and the government strictly administered imports. Consequently, an underground foreign exchange market flourished. The U.S. Dollar was selling at twice its official rate.

There was a critical shortage of construction materials. The resulting housing problem in major urban centers was something unheard of in the past. Demand outstripped supply once the housing industry became a state monopoly. The housing monopoly was supposedly to protect those of low income against rising cost of housing. However, rising costs of construction and growth in demand resulted in a permanent shortage of housing. The increase in population and the low-rent accommodation policy were the main reasons for the sharp increase in the demand for housing. At the same time, inflation raised both the costs of construction of new housing and maintenance of existing ones. Consequently, the Government's construction business accounted for over 50 percent of the total capital investment. Given the precipitous decline in the gross domestic savings ratio (11.8% in 1965–73, 6% in 1973–80 and 2.2% in 1980–86), the country faced a serious shortage of capital. Most of the capital equipment in manufacturing enterprises was worn out and obsolete. The flow of direct investment to Ethiopia almost ceased after 1978.

Priority for bank credit was given to public enterprises and budgetary deficits. Small producers borrowed funds from moneylenders at high rates due to bureaucratic red tape and insufficient credit at the state-owned banks. Because of the banking monopoly and absence of a securities market, it was not possible to mobilize domestic and external resources.

The record of the public enterprises was a mixed bag. With the exception of the state farms, the public enterprises operated at moderate profit levels. However, a number of public enterprises were facing rising debt, inefficient management and cumbersome bureaucracy. The State farms had been in trouble from the beginning.

The socialist system did not bring about material improvement. Instead, it hampered the private sector from growing, which did not create a favorable consequence for the economy. Dissatisfaction with the Stalinist regime of Mengistu Hailemariam mounted due to endless shortages of basic goods, the escalating cost of living and rising unemployment. The Regime had been caught in a vicious power struggle both within and without since its inception. The country got drawn more and more into superpower rivalry and regional power struggles. The Regime allied with the Soviet Union and drew the country deeper into superpower rivalry. Ethiopia's defense spending as a percentage of total expenditure increased from 14.3 percent in 1972 to 35.5 percent by the 1980s.[61] The Regime devoted its resources to fighting Tigrayan rebels in the north and teaching the population Marxist-Leninist ideology rather than investing in infrastructure and rewarding work to improve the economy. People destroyed one another engaging in government-sponsored so-called class struggle. The country lost its productive capabilities and traditional cohesiveness. The economy became more fragile and famine struck the north again in 1984/85.

The Government's response to the famine was to relocate the peasants from the north to the south, and to speed up cooperative villages in the countryside. In 1984, the Government launched a massive relocation program to transfer peasants from the drought-stricken, overpopulated north to the southwest, where there was adequate rainfall, fertile soil and lower population density. Relocation was seen by the Government as the only way to prevent famine from recurring in the future. By 1984, over 40 percent of the rural population had been relocated and villagized, with 100 percent villagization in the Harrarghe and Bale regions. The plan was to villagize the entire rural population (90 percent of the population of Ethiopia) by 1990.

Relocation was a high-cost operation. Each village consisted of as many as 500 families. It cost about 10,000 Ethiopian Birr to resettle each peasant family. Administrative overhead alone accounted for 43 percent of the total expenditure, infrastructure 23 percent, farm structures 16 percent, support costs 11 percent, capital outlay 5 percent and transportation and food costs 2 percent. The resettlement cost should also include the income from previous farms, lost due to the relocation. Villagization did not yield any benefit as such. Instead, it reduced rural labor productivity by 30 to 40 percent and displaced some six million people.

By 1990, the Regime realized its socialist policy was not working and announced a new policy of mixed economy that consisted of the state, cooperatives and the private sector.[62] This was not a change of heart, but a change of strategy for survival. According to the new policy, the state would continue to play a dominant role in organizing the economy as the sole proprietor of land. Central planning would be combined with market mechanisms to guide the economy. The State, cooperatives and private entrepreneurs would participate in all sectors of the economy. State enterprises would be given management autonomy and would work for profit. Private entrepreneurs would be allowed to develop commercial farms by leasing land from the state.

The new policy would open up the housing industry and import-export trade to the private sector. It would encourage partnership between domestic and foreign entrepreneurs and lift ceilings imposed on private investment. Inefficient state enterprises would either be sold to the private sector or closed down. Peasants would be given heritable use rights to land. They would own the produce and tree crops grown on their farms. The hiring of farm labor would be allowed. There would be a free market for grains. Small producers' cooperatives would be strengthened, and members would be allowed to dissolve their cooperatives if it were to their advantage to do so.

The policy was a replica of the Gorbachev reform program that tried to create a "third way" between the market economy and the command system. At the time, this did not work for the Soviets. The Eastern European countries that had rejected the brutal Soviet system and embraced democracy and the market economy had got off to a good start.

Tigrayan Dominance and the Post-Cold War Period

In May of 1991, shortly after the new policy was passed, the Tigrayan rebel army drove the Stalinist regime of Mengistu Hailemariam out of power. Eritrea split from Ethiopia, and the map of Ethiopia was redrawn along ethnic lines known as kilil, a formula for more sorrow, hate and cruel civil war.

In December of 1991, the new regime of Meles Zenawi issued an economic policy that was identical to that passed by the Stalinist regime of Mengistu Hailemariam on March 6, 1990. According to the economic policy of the new regime, the State would continue to own all land and essential sectors of the economy. Banking, insurance and telecommunication industries would not be open to foreign entrepreneurs. The state would offer 99-year leases on land, but not private ownership. Privatization measures would be undertaken and the private sector would be given more encouragement. Peasants would be allowed to lease use rights and hire farm labor. Land alienation through sale or mortgage in order to obtain improvement capital would not be allowed.[63]

The kilil policy created a new barrier for the private sector by fragmenting the national market and inhibiting the free movement of labor, capital and entrepreneurs. People divided themselves into indigenous and naftanyas (settlers) and started to fight for territory rather than equal rights. In ethnic territories, the kilil policy discriminated against so-called naftanyas and equal citizenship was denied. Most of the naftanyas moved to Addis Ababa and other towns with their labor and capital in order to survive. In the ethnic territories, checkpoints (reminiscent of nineteenth century Ethiopia) were used to control trade in grains, coffee and chat.

Independent merchants and entrepreneurs were locked out of the market through systematic discrimination and favoritism. Private entrepreneurs had to compete against the government's monopoly and party-owned businesses. Eritrean merchants, before the falling-out, enjoyed free access to Ethiopian markets, where they undersold local merchants. Most of so-called privatized businesses and land leases went to party-owned businesses and cronies who were unfairly favored by the government and lacked neither funds nor political clout. On the other hand, the state-owned Commercial Bank of Ethiopia charged private entrepreneurs and independent merchants prohibitive rates and required up to 100 percent of loan value to be secured by collateral.[64]

By mid-1992, the government implemented the structural adjustment program supported by loans from the International Monetary Fund (IMF).[65] Fifteen years later, Ethiopia is still poor with a per capita income of less than

$200. Government reports boast high growth rates fueled by government spending. But the production structure has not responded well because it is inflexible and rigid. The value of the Birr has declined. This should have stimulated exports, but production has not increased enough to feed the growing population, much less to export. Ethiopia is experiencing a huge population explosion accompanied by low purchasing power. Depreciation of the Birr has simply contributed to consumer price hikes. A daily laborer, if he is lucky, makes $1.00 a day. For the majority of the population, prices of most goods are untouchable. The lucky ones live off transfers from relatives living abroad. Retail prices of food grains doubled and prices of basic goods have increased by two-and-half to three times between 2001 and 2007.[66]

Oil price hikes have further depressed economic activities and pushed the cost of living through the roof. Small businesses are hurting from a value-added-tax (VAT) of 15 percent (2 to 3 times higher than the sales tax in the USA) and bureaucratic red tape. The burden of the VAT in retail businesses falls on the sellers because of the low purchasing power of the population. The government leases land at lucrative rates and pockets the money. Most of the big buildings and neighborhood homes still belong to the government. These buildings and homes are decaying due to massive neglect. There are new high rises and residential homes in Addis Ababa that are privately owned and are kept in good condition.

There is still a serious shortage of housing in Addis Ababa. The supply of housing lags behind due to shortages of building materials and mortgage loans. Import of materials is filling some of the gap and consequently, the increased expenditure is leaking to the outside world instead of stimulating domestic production and income. It takes two to three years to build a house in Addis Ababa. The owner has to provide most of the financing out of pocket because land is leased but not privately owned; it cannot be used as collateral to borrow money from banks. Bank loans are available for finishing a house by using the structure as collateral.

The government collects the bulk of its revenue from Addis Ababa, yet it is not investing adequately in the infrastructure of the city. There are power outages and shortages of water and telephone services. The telecommunication industry is a state monopoly and the government is the only internet service provider, hampering private entrepreneurs from using information technology to lower transaction costs and improve the economy.

Addis Ababa has recently seen several new roads, but public buildings, old streets and parks are not adequately maintained. City garbage is not collected properly. The pollution due to the smog from factories, leaded fuel and open sewers is unbearable, especially during the hot season. Traffic rules and conventional courtesy are not observed and order is noticeably lacking almost everywhere. The majority of the people in Addis Ababa live in squalid conditions without indoor plumbing and adequate sanitation. Infectious diseases and AIDS continue to take a heavy toll on lives.

The government has launched a program of building new universities, yet Addis Ababa University has deteriorated. The libraries are in disrepair and poorly equipped. There is hardly a decent chalkboard or desk in the classrooms. There are no overhead projectors let alone computers in the classrooms. The faculty and staff are underpaid and demoralized. The student body is ethnically divided and isolated.

Addis Ababa University does not look like an institution of higher learning where students go to satisfy their intellectual curiosity and dream about a promising future. A university is where everything begins. Without a strong university, it will be difficult to introduce new ideas into the country. Ethiopia will have an unproductive and unenlightened citizenry, afflicted by poverty, crimes and other social ills. Ethiopia will be unable to compete effectively in the world market and improve the well-being of its population.

One does not have to go far to see the seriousness of this problem. In South Africa during the Apartheid regime, the government purposely ignored investing in Black education. Blacks made up 70 percent of the population, but the ratio of per capita expenditure on education between Whites and Blacks was 4 to 1. Because of the color-based system that neglected investment in Black education, South Africa is today grappling with horrendous problems in the Black community. It has a shortage of skilled Black labor, limiting the introduction of new technologies. There is a high rate of unemployment among Blacks. Alcoholism, crimes and the AIDS crisis are hitting the Black community hard.

The problem of Addis Ababa University cannot be seen in isolation. The University is under the direct control of the government. It could not charge a tuition that is within the reach of Ethiopians of average financial means. It cannot create endowments that provide dependable support. It cannot solicit gifts from business, industry, alumni and other individuals that could be invested in plant, laboratory equipment and instructional technologies, such as computers and the internet. All these could help the University enjoy the benefits of information technology.

Information technology is so vital for education that the government in the United States, for instance, implements the internet in every public school but Ethiopia cannot put even a college student on the internet. Through internet accessibility, students and faculty in Ethiopia could browse, download and publish information worldwide. Compiling specific area of information into a computer media could help create an electronics library. Through video teleconferencing, distance learning could be made available to students in Ethiopia. Lectures could be recorded on a digital format and played for students on a computer training video. Furthermore, a wide range of degree programs could be offered on line. The internet could also reduce transaction costs for businesses. It could create employment opportunities in the information technology field. All this could propel Ethiopia into the information age of limitless opportunities.

Looking back at the history of Ethiopia's development shows that the political elite always rise to power by amassing military might. Once in power, the rulers dominate the rest of the society with their military might and appropriate the economic surplus for the purpose of pursuing elite status and self-preservation. The rulers, jealous of rivalry from their own entrepreneurs, centralize the lucrative economy in the hands of the Government and discriminate against, even persecute domestic entrepreneurs. The worst form of such a government occurred during the Stalinist Regime of Mengistu Hailemariam. Despite all this, the domestic entrepreneurs, the majority of them Gurage, have managed to create wealth for themselves and the rest of the society. The Gurage have a different mentality and contribute disproportionately to the economic development of Ethiopia. They are just four percent of the Ethiopian population yet they account for fifty-five to sixty percent of the business activities in Addis Ababa alone. In the following chapters, we will examine Gurage entrepreneurial success and its lessons of peace and development.

NOTES

1. Meier and Baldwin, *Economic Development Theory, History, Policy* (New York: Krieger Publishing Company, 1976) 246–247.

2. Walton and Robertson, *History of the American Economy* (New York: Harcourt Brace Jovanovich, Inc., 1983) 242–244. Harry Magdoff. "Capital, Technology and Development." *Monthly Review Press,* (January, 1976) 9–10.

3. Alec Nove, *An Economic History of the USSR* (Baltimore: Penguin Books, 1975) 11–28.

4. Marshall I. Goldman, *USSR in Crisis The Failure of an Economic System* (New York: W.W. Norton & Company, 1983).*The Margin*, Vol. 3. No. 1 (September, 1987) 6.

5. Franklin W. Houn, *A Short History of Chinese Communism* (Englewood Cliffs, New Jersey: Prentice Hall, Inc., 1973) 5–6.

6. Edgar Snow, *Red China Today* (New York: Random House, 1970) 62–63.

7. Jan S. Hogendorn, *Economic Development* (New York: Harper and Row, Publishers, 1987) 57–59.

8. Loehr and Powelson, *The Economics of Development and Distribution* (New York: Harcourt Brace Jovanovich, Inc. 1981) 387.

9. Walter Rodney, *How Europe Underdeveloped Africa* (Washington, D.C. Howard University Press, 1982).

10. Africa Institute of South Africa, *Africa At a Glance* (1992 and 1995/6).

11. Jan S. Hogendorn, *Economic Development*, 60.

12. Paul Prebish, "Commercial Policy in the Underdeveloped Countries" in *American Economic Review* (May, 1959) 251–27373. Gunnar Myrdal, *Rich Lands and Poor: The Road to World Prosperity* (New York: Harper and Row, 1957).

13. Jan S. Hogendorn, *Economic Development*, 60.

14. Jan S. Hogendorn, *Economic Development,* 60.

15. Jan S. Hogendorn, *Economic Development,* 60.

16. Loehr and Powelson, *The Economics of Development and Distribution,* 394–399.

17. See the statement by the late Julius Nyerere of Tanzania in P. T. Bauer, *Reality and Rhetoric: Studies in the Economics of Development* (Cambridge: Harvard University Press, 1984) 79.

18. See The Politics of Foreign Assistance in *Africa Report* (May-June, 1980) 50.

19. Michael P. Todaro, *Economic Development* (New York: Longman., 1994) 459.

20. Dominick Salvatore, *International Economics* (New York: Macmillan, 1993) 659.

21. Margery Perham, *The Government of Ethiopia* (Evanston: Northwestern University Press, 1969) 10–30. John Spencer Trimingham, *Islam in Ethiopia* (London: Frank Cass & Co, 1965) 32–42. Jones and Monroe, *A History of Ethiopia* (Oxford: Oxford University Press, 1935) 23, 26–31.

22. Jean Doresse, *Ethiopia* (London: Elek Books Ltd., 1956) 33. Margery Perham, *The Government of Ethiopia,* 19–21. Jones and Monroe, *A History of Ethiopia,* 33, 45, 46. John Spencer Trimingham, *Islam in Ethiopia,* 43, 44, 47–48 & 60.

23. Ethiopia's relation with the Christian world at this time was through the Coptic Church of Egypt at Alexandria. But the Coptic Church, working in collaboration with the Muslim rulers of Egypt, sometimes appointed abunas, bishops, who promoted Islamic interests in Ethiopia. Trimingham, *Islam in Ethiopia,* 48 & 60. Jones and Monroe, *A History of Ethiopia,* 52–59.

24. Trimingham, 52–59.

25. John Spencer Trimingham, *Islam in Ethiopia,* 58 & 67.

26. John Spencer Trimingham, *Islam in Ethiopia,* 62–68, 182–186. Richard Pankhurst, *An Introduction to Economic History of Ethiopia* (London: Staples Printers Ltd., 1961) 374.

27. Edward Ulendorff, "Gurage Notes."

28. John Spencer Trimingham, *Islam in Ethiopia,* 186.

29. Trimingham, *Islam in Ethiopia,* 190.

30. Max Gruhl, *Abyssinia at Bay* (London: Hurst and Blackett Ltd., 1935) 230.

31. Max Gruhl, *Abyssinia at Bay*, 229–232. Trimingham, *Islam in Ethiopia*, 14. Margery Perham, *The Government of Ethiopia, 317–322.*

38   *Chapter One*

32. Jean Doresse, *Ethiopia,* 115, 120–121. John Spencer Trimingham, *Islam in Ethiopia*, 47, 65, 71, 74 & 79.

33. John Spencer Trimingham, *Islam in Ethiopia*, 85–90. Jean Doresse, *Ethiopia,* 122, 128, 145. Jones Monroe, *A History of Ethiopia,* 102.

34. Trimingham, *Islam in Ethiopia,* 96, 129.

35. Mordechai Abir, *The Era of the Princes: The Challenge of Islam and the Reunification of the Christian Empire 1769–1855* (New York: Praeger Publishers, 1968) 9–14.

36. Trimingham, *Islam in Ethiopia,* 120, 124, 129.

37. Trimingham, *Islam in Ethiopia,* 129, 133–135.

38. Trimingham, *Islam in Ethiopia,* 102–104.

39. Jean Doresse, *Ethiopia,* 179–189. Richard Pankhurst, *An Introduction to Economic History of Ethiopia,* 317. Trimingham, *Islam in Ethiopia,* 103.

40. Trimingham, *Islam in Ethiopia,* 92–94.

41. A gada was a patriarchal age-grade group. Each community consisted of ten age groups or grades divided into two segments (half cycle) of five gadas each. Every mature male entered the segment, where his grandfather belonged, to become a member of his age group. Every eight years, the members of each gada moved to the next stage (gada) within their respective segment until they reached the stage of the ruling gada, where they would elect their leader, Aba Bochu, father of the sceptre, who would replace the outgoing leader. Upon the election of the new Aba Bochu, the old Aba Bochu and his gada would retire. The Aba Bochu was supported with voluntary tributes from his people during his tenure of office. With the decline of the gada system, the Aba Bia, a new class of landed proprietors emerged. The leader of the landed elite was the Moti, the King.

42. Trimingham, *Islam in Ethiopia,* 212–213.

43. Mordechai Abir, *The Era of the Princes,* 73–94. Trimingham, *Islam in Ethiopia,* 199–205.

44. Mordechai Abir, *The Era of the Princess,* 54–55.

45. Herbert Lewis, "A Reconsideration of the Socio-Political Systems of the Western Galla," in *Journal of Semetic Studies*, Vol. 9, No. 1, Spring (1964) 141–142.

46. Mordechai Abir, *The Era of the Princes,* 27–43. Trimingham, *Islam in Ethiopia, 193–198.*

47. Mordechai Abir, *The Era of the Princes,* 27–43. Trimingham, *Islam in Ethiopia, 193–198.*

48. Mordechai Abir, 27–43. Trimingham, 193–198.

49. Mordechai Abir, 27–43. Trimingham, 193–198.

50. Richard Pankhurst, *Economic History of Ethiopia 1800–1935* (Addis Ababa: Haile Selassie I University Press, 1968) 137–138.

51. Harold Marcus, *A History of Ethiopia* (Berkeley & Los Angeles: University of California Press, 1994) 114–115.

52. Jean Doresse, *Ethiopia,* 195. Trimingham, *Islam in Ethiopia,* 108.

53. Plowden in Richard Pankhurst, *Economic History of Ethiopia,* 9.

54. Jones and Monroe, *A History of Ethiopia,* 134–135.

55. Trimingham, *Islam in Ethiopia, 122.* Margery Perham, *The Government of Ethiopia,* 147.

56. Richard Pankhurst, *Economic History of Ethiopia.*

57. Jones and Monroe, 150–151.

58. Margery Perham, 181.

59. Margery Perham, 198, 232 & 292. Trimingham, 137 & 184. Italian Library of Information, "Development of Italian East Africa," New York: (n.d.), 37–48, 55–62, & 67.

60. For this and the information below, see Daniel Teferra, "Performance of Ethiopia's Socialist Economy," *A Discussion Roundtable on Ethiopia*, The Orkand Corporation, Silver Spring, MD, (November 9, 1989).

61. The World Bank. *World Development Report.* (1989 & 1997) 184 & 240 respectively.

62. *Sertoader,* Yekatit 29, 1982.

63. Tamrat Lyne, Prime Minister. "Ethiopia's Transitional Period Economic Policy Draft," in Amharinya, (Nehassie, 1983).

64. *The Economist*, (May 6th, 1995) 46, and information based on an interview with some members of the business community in Addis Ababa.

65. International Monetary Fund, *Press Release*, No. 96/51.

66. Daniel Teferra, "Ethiopia: Post-Cold War Market Reform and Globalization" in *PanEthiopia Forum*, Volume 2, Issue 1, 2000–2001 and based on the author's survey conducted in 2007.

Chapter Two

Entrepreneurship and Economic Development

God did not create rich people and poor people. He created all people. He created work. He created indolence. Work created wealth. Indolence created poverty. Creating and maintaining wealth is difficult. It creates a responsibility. It requires patience, tolerance, wisdom and frugality. Poverty is not difficult because it requires none of that. Poverty is wasteful. Poverty is destructive.

—Kenyazmach Teka Egeno

ORIGINS OF ENTREPRENEURSHIP

Economic development occurs when there is a widespread and steady improvement in the standard of living of a given society. This requires that more and more people learn and identify with entrepreneurial attitude, thereby engaging in wealth creation.

Entrepreneurial behavior is not randomly distributed throughout the population of any given country. In every case that has been studied, it has existed disproportionately in a single social group that is distinguished fairly sharply from other groups of the society.[1] Similarly in African countries disproportionate numbers of certain communities, such as the Ibo of Nigeria, Luo of Kenya or the Gurage of Ethiopia possess entrepreneurial behavior: they believe in the dignity of work, cooperation, frugality and material improvement through independent action. Historically, these groups through their customary drive have worked hard and acquired wealth and thereby made important contributions to the economic development of their respective societies.

Several theories have been advanced about entrepreneurial behavior. Max Weber believed that entrepreneurial behavior was a direct result of the Protestant ethic, especially Calvinism. He argued that the Protestant Dissenters in England brought about the Industrial Revolution because their religion taught them that the duty of human beings is to glorify God by making the earth fruitful. According to Weber, each member of the Dissenting sects worked unceasingly to be a "good tree" that will bring forth "good fruit," thereby gaining eternal salvation.[2]

Weber was correct in thinking that the Protestant Dissenters were leaders in the Industrial Revolution. However, he was wrong in asserting that their religion was the unique cause of their entrepreneurial talent. Entrepreneurial ability exists among Jews, Budhists, Muslims and many other religious groups.[3]

David C. McClelland, on the other hand, ascribes entrepreneurial behavior to achievement motivation, or need for achievement. He suggests that parents giving their children emotional rewards for independent action at an early age inculcate achievement motivation. He argues that the Protestant Dissenters were high achievers not as a result of their religion, but because the concern that a child should be destined for salvation caused parents to insist on early independent action. High achievement motivation necessarily finds expression in economic development, according to McClelland. Social scientists concerned with personality formation agree that differences among individuals in achievement motivation are real, important and associated with achievement, though not necessarily economic development.[4]

Everett E. Hagen, a development economist, believes that derogation is a source of entrepreneurial behavior and leads to innovation. He sketches a broad historical argument that the sense that leading groups of the same blood and general culture look down upon some group creates within that group a home atmosphere—a concern that children should be capable so that they can overcome or discount the derogation. In almost every society there is social derogation of some important group, which is leading technical progress and economic development, although a definite statement cannot be made without examining each case separately.[5]

The Gurage, for instance, have a different attitude from the rest of Ethiopia. They have work ethic. They are frugal and cooperate among themselves. They contribute disproportionately to economic development relative to their small numbers. The Gurage are not racially different from the other groups of Ethiopia. Their entrepreneurship, therefore, could be attributable to their specific history and socioeconomic institutions that have endured over time.

HISTORICAL BACKGROUND OF THE GURAGE

The Gurage, a very industrious people, live all over Ethiopia. They come from the fertile and mountainous region in southwestern Ethiopia and constitute about 4 percent of the total population of the country. The Gurage consist of four major subgroups: Ya sabat bet Gurage (Gurage of Seven Houses or Tribes) in the west, Masqan in the east, Soddo Kistane in the north, and Silte in the south (see Map 1.1).

The Chaha, Ezha, Geyto, Muher, Ennemor, Maqorqor and Endagany make up the Seven Houses. The Gurage have a common culture and language, spoken in three different dialects: eastern, western and northern. There are three types of believers among the Gurage: Christians, Muslims and followers of indigenous faiths.

The Gurage are descendants of Tigrayans from Gur'a (in present-day Akkele Guzay, in Eritrea) and the Sidama. They came in contact with the Christian Amhara, who mixed with them, influencing their language and religion.[6] The Gurage did fight among themselves in their history and invaded other groups. The Gurage had suffered historically from enemy raids and enslavement. They had fought against the Sidama, Oromo, Hadya and Amhara because each had attempted to wrest away their land and force them into slavery.[7]

The economy in the Gurage region is based on mixed agriculture and trade. Highland Gurage grows various types of cereals and vegetables. The lowland area grows enset (named false banana by foreign travelers), coffee, tobacco, chat, corn and root crops.[8]

The main product of the enset plant is the fiber-rich kocho, the fermented starch of the pseudo-stem and the corm, which is the staple food of the Gurage and other Sidama groups. Kocho does not spoil easily and can be preserved in the ground for several years. Starvation and famine were unknown in Gurage history thanks, in part, to the enset plant.

Women who know the trade well extract kocho from enset. First the corms and tissues of the pseudo-stem of a mature enset are cut up and fermented for a certain period of time, ranging from a few weeks to one or more years. The longer the product has fermented, the more it is appreciated. The fermented product is pressed to remove the acid fermentation liquid and the dough-like remnant is mixed with salt and baked into pieces of bread, which are then eaten with cooked greens, beef stew or kitfo (finely chopped beef mixed with spiced butter, salt and cardamom). The finer dough is called bula and is used for making bread. Bula is also boiled and eaten as porridge, mixed with salt, and spiced butter and berbere (hot pepper). The fresh corms, or hamicho (in Sidama), are also eaten, cooked with cabbage. The Gurage have successfully commercialized kocho and are the major suppliers to the Addis Ababa market.

In addition to serving the nutritional needs of the Gurage, enset serves many other purposes. The pseudo-stems provide fiber for making ropes, baskets and rugs. Enset leaves are used for wrapping food items, covering roofs and as bedding materials.

The Gurage have occupied their present territory for many centuries. Each Gurage subgroup (Bete Gurage) was organized to the village level under a system known as Sera with its own administrative rules and laws. At the top of the Sera was an elected Azmach (Imam for Muslims), meaning chief or king, who enforced the rules and laws, assisted by elders. The seven subgroups that formed Ya sabat bet Gurage Hibret (Seven Houses of Gurage Cooperation) for peace and unity had one Sera called Yejoka Sera. Although each Gurage subgroup had its own Sera, the administrative rules and laws of the subgroups were (and still are) very similar.[9]

The Gurage had made significant political, social and economic advances before they were incorporated into the Ethiopian Empire by conquest between 1875 and 1889.[10] Before the coming of imperial rule, the Gurage had controlled violence and learned how to cooperate and lead a productive life. They knew how to earn income working as skilled artisans, migrant laborers and long distance traders; consequently, they had become judicious in commerce and handling money. They were mobile and moved freely, looking for

Azmach Bantawi and the author

work and investment opportunities. "The Gurage merchants go to Setshiro, a district of the Wolamo tribe," wrote a foreign traveler, "and receive dirgo (wages) from the king till they return to their country."[11]

Through migrant labor and long distance trade, the Gurage were able to develop a relatively good relationship with the other ethnic groups. They opened their markets to the Amhara, Sidama, Oromo, Kambata, Janjero and other groups. Surrounded by warring Oromo and Sidama groups that threatened their existence and movement, the Gurage survived by making pacts "which prevented hostilities from taking place within the market area and guaranteed safe conduct for their traders en route."[12]

Although land provided social and economic security, the Gurage relied on trade and wage labor to achieve this aim more quickly and to tackle the population-resource imbalance. Hence, adult males migrated to other places in large numbers during the agricultural off-season in search of employment opportunities. This not only provided income, but also helped the Gurage to become risk takers and independent.[13]

In the late nineteenth century, the Shawan conquest under Menelik imposed the gult (fief) system on the Gurage. The Gurage were forced to give up their fertile land and live under onerous obligations.[14] The Gurage fought gallantly to defend their country against Menelik's invasion. It took fourteen years for the Shawans to defeat the Gurage. The Gurage mention with pride their victory over the Shawan army at Areket in Gumer. It took Menelik three expeditions (he led the third one himself) to finally subdue the Gurage.[15]

Despite the imperial incorporation, the Gurage continued to rely on their Sera system and Yejoka. Thus Gogot, the peace and unity vow of all the Gurage people, was modeled by the early twentieth century after Yejoka, which still serves as the judicial council of elders of all the Gurage subgroups to settle intra- and inter-subgroup disputes.

The Shawan gult system hastened land scarcity and accelerated the migration of the Gurage to Addis Ababa and other centers.[16] The Gurage used their entrepreneurial experience to take advantage of a wider market and meet the challenges and opportunities presented by the imperial incorporation. They forged ahead economically.

The gult system was abolished during the brief Italian occupation of Ethiopia. This gave the Gurage an opportunity to reorganize their society under their own system. The Italians encouraged road construction, creating further incentives for wage labor and migration of the Gurage to Addis Ababa.[17] The Italians favored their own merchants and discriminated against the Gurage. They pitted the Gurage merchants against the others, separating them by ethnicity and religion.

Upon independence in 1941, the imperial system was restored and the gult system was brought back until it was abolished completely in 1966. The Gurage migration to Addis Ababa and other major cities increased rapidly after the Second World War during the second reign of Haile Selassie (1941–1974). The Gurage did any kind of work and competed successfully with Greek, Armenia, Arab and Indian merchants who had controlled business in Addis Ababa and other urban centers (see Appendix I). By the late 1960s and early 1970s, the Gurage dominated most of the trading and manufacturing activities of the Markato, the central market in Addis Ababa. Gurage progress, however, was suppressed with selfish cruelty by the Stalinist regime of Mengistu Hailemariam (1975–1991). The Gurage had to survive by joining the informal economy.

In 1991, the Mengistu Hailemariam regime was toppled and the new Regime of Meles Zenawi relaxed some of the restrictions on the market. This gave the Gurage a chance to regroup. But the new regime raised business taxes, increased rent on shopping centers and created party-owned businesses to control the private sector. The Government's kilil (ethnic-based) policy fragmented the market, thereby hampering free movement of labor, capital and entrepreneurs.[18]

Areket and its surroundings, Gumer, Gurage

Table 2.1. Percentage Distribution of Business Ownership by Ethnic Group Addis Ababa, 2004.

Type of Business	% Owned by Gurage	% of Gurage Population	% Owned by Others	Population % of Others
Restaurant	80	4.0	20	96.0
Hotel & Motel	40	4.0	60	96.0
Import/Export	40	4.0	60	96.0
Leather Prod.	60	4.0	40	96.0
Metal Prod.	50	4.0	50	96.0
Farm Related	50	4.0	50	96.0
Flour Mills	70	4.0	30	96.0
Retail	60	4.0	40	96.0

Source: Based on the author's survey.

The Zenawi regime held a monopoly over land and lucrative sectors of the economy. It gave party-owned businesses preferential treatment. The Gurage entrepreneurs used their experience to open new areas of business and excelled the party-owned businesses. They made their presence felt once again in the private sector.[19] The Gurage are now back in the saddle in Addis Ababa (see Table 2.1).

GURAGE WORK ETHIC AND FRUGALITY

"One person alone cannot save. One person alone cannot create wealth. One has to live within his means. Money will vanish easily unless it is invested. Water and money will disappear unless more and more is added to what already exists. It is impossible to survive unless the rains feed the rivers and people keep adding to the wealth that they already have." the late Ato Dambel Shai.

The Gurage are known for their work ethic and frugality. The two institutions primarily responsible for this are family and community. The Gurage value family. The dignity of work and independence are taught at an early age. Children are exposed to life lessons when they are young. They start taking orders from their parents when they are just five. A close child-parent relationship begins at this time. The father disciplines his son with words of wisdom and teaches him about life. The Gurage do not believe in physical punishment. If the father has to discipline the child, he will do so by pinching slightly the ear of the child with his two fingers.[20]

When a girl turns eight, her mother teaches her all about household chores; by the time she is ten she will do the domestic activities by herself without her mother's supervision. She learns from her mother about cooking, home-brewing, basketry, jewelry making and hairdressing.[21]

Children grow up seeing their parents do any kind of work in order to raise them; consequently, they feel a sense of responsibility to work and help their parents and themselves. A Gurage child puts the well-being of his/her parents above all else. The community treats a child who helps his/her parents and receives their blessing with high esteem. To be a good child is to receive the blessing of one's parents.

The Gurage community plays a major role in promoting the work ethic. The community considers begging shameful; therefore the Gurage do not beg. Shepherds in Gurage used to sing a song called Warsie to mock the lazy and discourage loitering and indolence.[22] The Gurage have a saying that glorifies the value of work: "zer ayifakim, sira ayinakim (family roots cannot be denied; no work can be despised."[23])

The Gurage community is all-inclusive. It embraces rich and poor alike. Consequently, the poor are not separated from opportunities. They are mentored and helped by the rich to find work and improve themselves. In this manner, the Gurage promote the work ethic and take care of one another.

Mentoring and networking promote the work ethic among the Gurage. For instance, kinsmen or close friends will assist a migrant worker upon his arrival in the city. He will be given accommodation and employment or the latest business information or training. He will be given credit if he wants to start his own business.[24] The Gurage view mentoring and networking as a social responsibility. This is clear as one traces the path of a Gurage from shoe-shiner to prominent entrepreneur. When a Gurage teenager first comes to Addis Ababa a mentor will take him under his wings and teach him how to earn income and become independent. Gurage teenagers are well behaved and goal oriented; therefore they do not involve themselves in criminal activities. Their main objective is to earn income and help their parents and themselves.[25]

The mentor will provide the teenager with shelter and shoe-shining equipment. The mentor will then link him up with other Gurage shoe-shiners who will help him learn the trade. The teenager spends the first few days observing the others at work. They give him minor assignments, a kind of apprenticeship training, to help him familiarize himself with the work and build up his self-confidence. After a few weeks he will start working independently and eventually he will support himself with his income, covering all his living expenses. When he returns home (Agerbet) for the Masqal (or Arafa if he is a Muslim) Holiday, the younger boys will emulate him because of his success and follow in his footsteps. It will now be his turn to mentor the new arrivals.

A Gurage works and saves patiently for up to ten years on average before moving to the next higher goal from shoe shining or working as an employee in a restaurant, shop, or tejbet (local bar). Then he opens his own kiosk, teashop, or tejbet. About 50 percent of the funds for starting new businesses

A shoe-shiner at work, Addis Ababa

come from personal savings. The Gurage have a high saving rate of 25 to 30 percent of income.[26] The remaining 50 percent of the funds come from Iqub (a lending cooperative) and family sources.

The Gurage are frugal because of their cooperative attitude and work ethic. They save to invest in productive activities and create wealth. They depend on one another to achieve this goal. For instance, the Gurage women form what is called Oujo to accumulate milk through individual contributions to produce butter. Churning the milk every three days produces the butter. There has to be a large quantity of milk to do this. But the amount of milk that each woman gets from her cow is not sufficient. If a small amount of milk is kept aside for the purpose of extracting butter, it will dry and lose flavor. The women bring their milk together to create a larger quantity. Then they produce the butter and divide it among themselves according to their contributions.[27] The women also form what is called Qib-yidemuji to save butter for special occasions. Each member contributes a specific amount of butter every week. The butter is stored at one place, usually at the house of an elderly member of the group. It will then be distributed when the special occasion arrives.[28]

In order to finance business activities, the Gurage form an Iqub, a lending cooperative. The Iqub collects funds periodically from members and allocates the money through a lottery system. Men, women and even children practice Iqub. A judge and a secretary administer the Iqub. Each member contributes

A Gurage street vendor, Addis Ababa

a fixed sum periodically. The contribution per member is called medeb (base). If each medeb is $100 and the sum of $5,000 is to be raised every week, for example, there will be 50 members in the Iqub. If a member chooses to have more than one medeb, then the number of members will be less than 50. A ticket is prepared bearing the name of each member. If someone has more than one medeb, his/her name appears on more than one ticket. The tickets will be rolled in front of the members before the drawing takes place. This process is repeated every week or month depending on when the lottery is drawn. The winner of the lottery will then collect the money upon producing a guarantor (sometimes up to three guarantors are required for a larger sum), who will be responsible in case the winner fails to make the periodic payments after having won the lottery. Each winning ticket is removed from the pot and destroyed.[29] The winner of the lottery has the right to collect his/her money or sell the winning ticket for profit to another member who may have an urgent financial need. In order to accommodate members who may have such needs, the sum can also be offered for sale to the members from time to time. The profit from the sale is divided among the members.[30]

Every income group practices Iqub. There is, for instance, Iqub for the low income with a minimum contribution of not less than five dollars. This is administered usually in the tejbet (local bar). An individual will be given a book and his daily contribution will be entered in it and signed by the Iqub judge and secretary. After a certain period of time, the individual will collect the accumulated sum upon paying a book fee.[31] There is also a holiday Iqub for the low income that is run the same way. The Wealthiest Iqub is the one that is practiced by prominent merchants with a contribution of up to $2,000 per month. Big hotels in the Markato, the central market in Addis Ababa, usually administer this kind of Iqub.[32]

The Gurage admire success and emulate one another. For instance, the next goal after a tejbet could be to own a flour-mill, a bakery, or a grocery store. Individuals move up the ladder of success all the way to opening a hotel, a restaurant, a supermarket, a department store, or a factory. The Gurage women join the ranks of entrepreneurs starting from a humble beginning working as traders in salt, berbere (hot pepper), spices, butter and cheese. By the late 1960s and early 1970s there were many successful Gurage entrepreneurs. They managed to wrestle most of the businesses in the Markato out of the hands of foreign residents.

Through their work ethic and frugality the Gurage have conquered hardship and poverty.[33] They have for centuries earned their livelihood as proficient farmers, traders and artisans. They have grown their own food, made "their own tools, farm implements and house wares and built their own homes."[34] They have mastered woodwork, metal work, pottery, carpentry, masonry, leatherwork and the production of straw and bamboo products[35] without any formal education or vocational training. They have long sold their products (hides and skin, coffee, kocho, chat, tobacco, berbere or hot pepper, butter, cheese, grains, cereals, pottery, woodworks, shama or local costume, buluko or heavy cotton blanket, basketry, fiber products, and so on) in local markets and long distance trade. They are mobile and have supplemented their farm incomes by working as migratory workers during off-seasons. Historically they have used commodities (salt bars, divided into sinaga, gadal, kirayu, losie) and precious metals (copper divided into natir, alad, drim, kafla) as mediums of exchange.[36]

The Gurage enjoyed an independent and promising development prior to their incorporation into the Ethiopian Empire in the late nineteenth century. They used their entrepreneurial experience and took advantage of a wider market to grow despite the conquest. Gurage artisans and laborers who were brought to Addis Ababa as captives by Emperor Menelik's army provided much of the labor needed in the palace workshop. The commercial establishments owned by Yemenites, Greeks, Armenians, Indians and Arabs hired some of them. Still many others migrated to Addis Ababa and took up trading and artisan activities, menial jobs and domestic service in the city.[37]

A Gurage grocer, Addis Ababa

The Gurage made up the largest portion of the labor force during the establishment phase of Addis Ababa in the late nineteenth century, working on construction of roads and houses as well as in various types of service activities. They supplied most of the produce to Addis Ababa by tending vegetable and fruit gardens on the outskirts of the city. They ran retail businesses in foodstuffs and other products. The Soddo Gurage, were the small tailors and artisans of Addis Ababa. They were involved in long distance trade in the extended empire working as commercial agents for the imperial elite.[38]

By the 1930s the Gurage were beginning to own retail stores in Addis Ababa although ownership of the industry was still dominated by foreign residents. Yet half the trading population of the city at this time was made up of the Gurage. They "conducted their business in the shops of other merchants on a rental basis and in a few cases on the basis of joint ownership. Many Gurage traders conducted their businesses in open stalls or booths."

By establishing good relationships with Indian merchants who dominated the import-export business, the wealthy Gurage retailers got direct access to imported raw materials for making shama or local costume. They also gained access to commercial vegetable production, a monopoly of the Armenians, Greeks and Italians, as well as penetrating the butchery and tailoring industries and the textiles trade. The Gurage became traders in cattle, hides and skins as well as producers and sellers of leather products. They put into practice the training and skills that they had acquired, working as employees and domestic service providers for foreign residents who dominated these areas.

This advance was briefly disrupted during the Italian occupation (1936–41). Gurage migrant workers benefited from employment opportunities in road construction, domestic services and menial jobs. However, the Italians dismantled the palace economy and introduced a new currency and a racist policy. They expelled foreign residents and brought in their own merchants. They discriminated against the Gurage and created rivalry and hatred between the Gurage and the Muslim merchants from Tigrai, Gondar, Gojjam, Wollo and Jimma. The Gurage merchants (Christians and Muslims alike) put up stiff competition despite the preferential treatment given to the other Muslim merchants. They capitalized on their extensive experience in the marketing of foodstuffs and other local products as the demand for these commodities increased significantly due to the large colonial population and influx of people to the city. Gurage merchants rented store sites and the number of Gurage shops in the Markato or central market in Addis Ababa increased. The Gurage merchants, particularly the Soddo Gurage, engaged in currency trade, exchanging Italian lire for the Maria Theresa, which was in great demand, especially in the countryside.

The post-independence period during the reign of Haile Selassie (1941–1974) saw unprecedented growth and development among the Gurage. In addition to their traditional fields of trade, they were involved in exporting hides and skins, cash crops such as coffee, and importing of capital and consumer goods: agricultural equipment, fertilizers, building materials, spare parts and household goods. They were involved in retail and wholesale trade, the hotel and restaurant industry, dry cleaning, pharmaceuticals and service stations. The Gurage established manufacturing enterprises, making shoes, sweaters, home and office furniture, drinks, as well as metal and glass products. They excelled in the clothing industry and jewelry making. They invested part of their profits in lucrative real estate in Addis Ababa. They invested in commercial agriculture, growing cash crops, such as, coffee, cotton and oil seeds as well as staple crops and cereals. They also took advantage of the opportunities presented by modern education during this time to become professionals in a wide range of fields. They served the government ably in different capacities, but they were mostly involved in the private sector, running their own businesses. They enjoyed the freedom of movement and the opportunity for building capital offered by the private sector.

The Gurage lost most of these advances during the Stalinist regime of Mengistu Hailemariam (1975–1991). The government abolished private property rights and confiscated everything from the smallest neighborhood store to the biggest firm. It imposed crippling restrictions on merchants and traders. Merchants were denied permits to import goods and were not allowed to farm privately. Having inventories on hand was considered a crime. A number of Gurage traders, merchants and entrepreneurs were imprisoned and had their goods confiscated. Some of them, including prominent entrepreneurs were publicly executed by the military rulers, who falsely blamed them for marketeering—called ashatir by the soldiers—and anti-revolutionary activities.[39] They were used as a scapegoat for the government's failed policy. The following excerpts from *Notes from the Hyena's Belly* by Nega Mezlekia illustrate the persecution of the Gurage by the Stalinist regime of Mengistu Hailemariam:

"There was a flourishing black market for food stuff, but only the very rich could afford to purchase any of the items. The army decided to help. The 'guilty' were brought out with their hands tied behind them. Most of them were merchants from the Gurage ethnic group who have earned a reputation as gifted entrepreneurs. Just after dawn, eleven men were lined up against those mute cliffs and shot dead. Some thought that the execution was a noble idea. As it turned out, the market dried up altogether. The ones who benefited from this drastic measure were the soldiers, who divided among themselves the confiscated goods, but after a while, as the supplies were eaten up, even they became victims of their poor judgement."[40]

Despite all this, the Gurage did not claim to be victims. They relied on their resilience and entered the informal market in order to survive. They began to compete with government stores in the neighborhoods, buying indirectly their merchandise in large quantities and retailing it in their kiosks and shops. Gurage kiosks were fully stocked while the government stores often displayed empty shelves. They created a market for government coupons, known as ayer-ba-yer. They purchased the coupons from government officials and sold them at a premium to the general public.[41]

When the Mengistu regime was toppled in 1991, some of the restrictions on the market were relaxed by the regime of Meles Zenawi, but new barriers were created. Because of the regime's kilil (ethnic-based) policy, merchants and entrepreneurs could not move freely, seeking work and investment opportunity. The government accused them of capitalist exploitation when they tried to invest in the countryside. Those who managed to get there were pushed out by the ethnic administration. The entrepreneur had no security for his life, much less his investment.[42]

In Addis Ababa, the regime of Meles Zenawi raised business taxes and rent on shopping centers; consequently, the cost of doing business skyrocketed for the Gurage. Furthermore, the government formed party-owned businesses, thereby creating ethnic bias and unfair competition. The party-owned businesses were accorded preferential treatment, importing goods easily (without paying taxes and proper invoicing) and enjoying government contracts without proper bidding. The Gurage responded by going into ventures unknown to party-owned businesses. Before long, most of the party-owned businesses turned out to be unprofitable. The Gurage then partnered with and bought out some of these businesses, thereby increasing their influence in the private sector.[43]

The government is still the major economic player and owns all land; it is not easy for the Gurage entrepreneurs to invest in real estate or commercial agriculture. Furthermore, the government's kilil policy works against their economic interest by fragmenting the national market. The Gurage are opposed to the kilil policy because it restricts their movement, limiting them to their own ethnic territory. One Gurage entrepreneur said, "No other group loves Ethiopia as much as we do. We made our money not in our territory, but by working all over Ethiopia."[44]

Most of the entrepreneurial activities of the Gurage are still concentrated in Addis Ababa. One can see in Addis Ababa today that more and more educated members of the Gurage community have joined the ranks of entrepreneurs, running big banks, insurance companies, factories, real estate and other major businesses (see Appendix II & III).

GURAGE COOPERATION

For the Gurage, cooperation is the source of their strength. Without cooperation, it would be difficult for the Gurage to ensure their continued success and security. The Gurage have institutions that promote cooperation by managing conflict and building trust. First, there is the family unit, where bonding and virtues of peace and a cooperative attitude are learnt at an early age. Second, there is the all-inclusive community that embraces all members without making any distinction between rich and poor. The community embraces the individual starting from birth. There is no alienation or isolation in the Gurage community. Third, there are various friendship associations that help the Gurage control aggressive tendencies and promote camaraderie. Finally, there is Yejoka, the uniquely Gurage institution that is largely responsible for influencing the social behavior of the Gurage.

The Gurage value family highly. A Gurage family is caring and loving. Parents and children form a close-knit unit. For Gurage parents, there is nothing more important than properly raising their children. They will do anything to earn income and raise their children. The mother breastfeeds her child for as long as three to four years, evidence that there is a strong bonding between parents and their children from the start. During the first four years, the father cares for the child gently without raising his voice or talking angrily. Parents often take their children with them wherever they go; and make sure that they are well fed when they are out with them.

The Gurage love children and a big family. They respect mothers and celebrate antrosht, mother's day, once a year by throwing a party for relatives and neighbors. When the number of children reaches eight, a party known as samin will be given in honor of the mother. When the number of children reaches ten, the celebration will be for as long as eight days. The Gurage appreciate their children too. There is children's day in the Gurage culture. On boys' day, games and feasts will be organized for the boys. On girls' day, girls will have a day off from household chores.[45]

Gurage children show great affection and respect for their parents. They put the well- being of their parents ahead of their own.[46] Love of parents and respect for elders are inculcated in the minds of Gurage children at an early age. The Gurage see one another as family. If two Gurages meet, the younger will approach the other and greet him by kissing him on his hands and shoulders.[47] Children bond with neighbors and family friends while growing up; consequently, they learn a sense of community. The titles of uncle and aunt are bestowed on male and female friends of the family. Children see their parents receive a blessing from elders for extending a helping hand in time of need. The Gurage believe that the blessing of their elders will make them successful in life; therefore, they always strive to live productive and peaceful lives.

The Gurage community is a strong and enduring community. It has its own customs, traditions and laws. In the first place, it gives the individual security and hope by embracing everyone without making any distinction between rich and poor. The Gurage do not turn their backs on one another. If a poor family does not have milk to raise a child, the neighborhood will take turns under a system called Oujo to provide milk to that child. When a child is born, the community sees it as its own. If someone in the neighborhood slaughters an animal, half of the meat will be sent to the new mother. If a woman loses her husband, the neighborhood will be ordered to bring dinner to the bereaved family. The men in the neighborhood look after the family's farm and herd for six months. During holidays or weddings, everyone, including children, has an assignment. The women draw water, grind grain and prepare the food, men take care of the dining area and children collect firewood.

The elders enforce the customs and traditions of the community. For instance, if someone fails to bring dinner to a bereaved family, first his jiba (a sleeping mat) will be removed from his house. If he fails a second time, the front door of his house will be removed. If he fails a third time, he will be excluded from the community. He will not be allowed to borrow anything from his neighbors. His cows will not be allowed to mix with the neighborhood herd. His children will not play with other children. His wife will not mix with other women.[48]

The Gurage share their happiness as well as their sorrow. It is a way of expressing respect for one another. When someone dies, survivors bury their dead and then request from the elders for the rule to mourn with the community. This will be granted if elders who know the bereaved testify that he/she is an honorable person who has served his/her parents well and received their blessing. The testimony is a serious matter. The elders take an oath: "We will speak the truth. If we do not speak the truth, may this loss befall us." Once the request is granted, no one will be denied the opportunity to pay his/her respect. Even criminals will be granted immunity for that day to pay their respects. The request to mourn will be denied if someone has not served his/her parents and consequently, has their curse on him/her.

The Gurage have long built friendship and trust among themselves. For instance, children call one another by love names, such as sakum (leader) for boys and agostie-adoyie or kantoyie-abitie for girls, as an expression of affection and respect. These childhood friendships are long lasting.

There are friendship associations such as Gurda that reinforce cooperation and trust among the Gurage. Gurda is a covenant of reciprocal obligation or mutual assistance between distantly related men. Gurda involves economic and social cooperation as well as protection against physical harm.[49]

Idir, neighborhood association, is another cooperative institution among the Gurage. The Gurage organize themselves by neighborhoods to take care of one another when there is death or other calamities in a member's family. They also help others in the community when they are in need of money to start a business or are faced with a financial crisis. Members of the same Idir contribute money, buy land and build their homes; they even buy shares in businesses. Through Idir, the Gurage also help the poor, the unemployed and the less fortunate.

Sera is another institution similar to Idir. Sera is undertake by neighbors. Those under one Sera are considered friends and have a moral obligation to respect the interest of one another. No one in a Sera will assist or conspire with an outsider to harm a Sera member. "Ahersh! Yina yessera sub anheneway?" (No! I cannot assist. We are under one Sera.). The Gurage also use Sera to present a united front on a specific issue, such as the question of dowry, marriage, or schooling children. On each of these issues, they will have YaGurage Sera and everyone will abide by it.[50]

The institution that most influences the social behavior of the Gurage is Yejoka. The Gurage had a long history of violence and destruction before they were able to achieve relative peace. Sibling rivalries, interfamilial conflicts, clan feuding and internecine warfare and enslavement were common among the Gurage. Criminal activities, such as theft, physical assault, arson and murder were widespread. In addition the Gurage had suffered repeatedly from external attacks and slave raiding by the Amhara, Oromo, Hadya, Sidama and other groups. The Gurage were small in numbers relative to most of their attackers. They were becoming even fewer due to internal subgroup competition and feuding. They were forced to come together and defend themselves as a matter of survival. Initially, the western Gurage subgroups of Chaha, Ezha, Muher, Ennemor and Geyto known as Ya Amist bet Gurage Hibret (Five Houses of Gurage Cooperation) took a peace and unity vow to stop fighting among themselves and "create a unified resistance against their common enemies." An attack on one subgroup was considered an attack on all of them. No subgroup could ally with an outside enemy to attack the Hibret.[51]

Over time, two more western subgroups of Maqorqor and Endagany were added to the Hibret. First, Maqorqor joined forming Ya Sidist bet Gurage Hibret (Six Houses of Gurage Cooperation).[52] Prior to this, Maqorqor had been a gateway for external enemies, such as the Oromo and Hadiya to attack the Five Houses. The Five Houses also used to go through Maqorqor to fight the Oromo groups of Amaya, Nadaro and Wolliso.[53] In order to close the southern flank from repeated attacks against Ennemor by the Konteb ethnic group, a seventh member—Endagany—was added to the Hibret and Ya Sabat bet Gurage Hibret (Seven Houses of Gurage Cooperation) was formed.[54]

The successful experience of Ya Sabat bet Gurage laid a firm foundation for lasting peace and unity among the entire Gurage community. As a result of the leadership and hard work of Sella Odda of Soddo Kistane, all Gurage subgroups took a peace and unity vow known as Gogot. The peace and unity vow prohibited subgroup feuding or allying with an outside enemy to attack the Gurage or any subgroup. If a subgroup attacks another subgroup, the other subgroups will get together and attack the perpetrator.[55]

The experience of Ya Sabat bet Gurage created for the Gurage a central institution that established a judicial and moral standard and set the tone for the social behavior of the entire community. Having isolated their external enemies and detractors, Ya Sabat bet Gurage used Yejoka or judicial council of elders to control internal feuding and promote cooperation. Yejoka was originally organized by an elder called Japiwa Geta of the Chaha subgroup to settle intra-ethnic and inter-clan disputes; consequently, the representatives of the Seven Houses all took part in it.

The judicial council was named after the Village of Yejoka, located in Chaha territory at Yabaze where the rituals of Yejoka were performed. Yejoka was (and still is) the most important judicial council of the Seven Houses of

Gurage.⁵⁶ It serves as the source of judicial and moral authority for Ya Sabat bet Gurage, lying above inter-clan councils, which in turn rank above village councils of elders. Yejoka "sets rules and establishes norms for proper social development of children, respect for elders and support for the aged, marriage and divorce, conflict resolution, controlling wasteful and harmful practices and respect for property."⁵⁷

The rules of Yejoka, known as Yejoka Kicha locally, promote peace and cooperation among the Gurage by influencing the behavior of every Gurage regardless of social or economic status. Intra-subgroup or inter-clan disputes, civil or criminal, were (and still are) settled by Yejoka. Yejoka rules prohibit all forms of oral and physical aggression and promote mutual respect and kindness toward one another among the Gurage. The rules have recently prohibited unnecessary practices, such as selest (wailing by close relatives three days after a funeral.) They abolished tazkar (a feast given in honor of the deceased). The Yejoka rules required an AIDS test before marriage. They made sure that Gurage migrant workers and traveling merchants showed AIDS test results before having conjugal contact with their wives upon returning home.⁵⁸ Ya Sabat bet Gurage and all other Gurage subgroups today observe Yejoka rules. Any serious inter-subgroup issue will be referred to Yejoka for settlement.⁵⁹

The Gurage subgroups had a long history of resolving disputes and promoting cooperation even before the coming of Yejoka. For instance, the Soddo Kistane used a system known as senecha in which a group of elders interceded to advise or even impose sanctions whenever there was any kind of criminal activity or anti-social behavior in the community. The elders were peace watchdogs of the community. They quickly brought conflicts under control through peaceful means.

The Gurage today rely mostly on their elders to settle family or business disputes. They respect their elders. For the Gurage, elders are "next to God"⁶⁰ because they are the protectors of the young and defenders of the community. They are well known for their fairness and sense of justice.⁶¹ Everyone is heard, rich or poor.

On matters of public concern, the elders speak first while the rest listen in silence without interruption. One can only speak when it is his/her turn. In addressing a meeting of the elders, everyone starts with words of blessing and praise: "Let the day be a blessed one. The tongue speaks the truth. Let us be forgiven for our mistakes. Let all kings be protected by their crowns. Long live the elders. Let the young grow. Let there be peace in our land. And let all who are here return to their respective homes in happiness."⁶²

Because peace is the premise of the Gurage elders, they always promote reconciliation and compromise. They discourage vengeance. For instance, in

The Yejoka Tree, Chaha, Gurage

the past when a murder was committed, the elders from both families used to intercede before the courts took up the case and reconcile the two families by seeking truth and forgiveness. They would seclude the alleged killer and his family from the sight of the victim's relatives while the case was being investigated. In Gurage history, capital punishment was discouraged unless in special circumstances such as arson. Revenge killing was prohibited. The execution of a convicted killer was carried out not by a relative of the victim but by one of the close male relatives of the convicted murderer himself.[63]

The Gurage elders are generally chosen for their wisdom rather than their economic or political status. They are wise men of the community. They are humble and respectful and lead by example. They take their responsibility seriously. They stand out because they resolve conflict by seeking truth, thereby avoiding continuation of conflicts. In their deliberation, they begin with such words as "Let the mouth speak blessed words. May God avoid murders and conflicts from Gurage. There are two things for which such a group of elders is gathered today, to speak the truth and handle the dispute."[64]

In settling a dispute, the elders ask the guilty to give ak (truth) to the victim. The guilty one accepts their decision, admits his guilt and says, "I give ak." Then they tell the victim, "You are truthful. The guilty has acknowledged his guilt. You have to receive ak." The victim accepts their decision, receives ak, and makes peace with the offender. The guilty one apologizes to the victim for his guilt. In case of a serious offense, compensation will be ordered in cash or kind. The victim can receive the payment or he may let the offender go free.[65]

The decisions of the elders are always respected. If someone defies their decision, they will give the violator several chances to appear before them to explain the reason. They send a delegation of four elders first. If there is no response, they will send another delegation of eight, then twelve. If there is still no response, they will impose sanctions. The violator could receive their curse and be excluded from the community. No member of the community will ever keep contact with the violator again.

The Gurage believe that the curse of their elders is real; it could happen to them. They do not wish to defy their elders. They do not want to lie or fail to live up to their commitments. There are no written contracts among the Gurage as such because they keep their word and trust one another.[66] They do not betray or abandon one another.

Although warfare and enemy raids have long disappeared, the Gurage still harbor apprehensions from past experience that physical harm or deprivation may come their way. They cannot expect protection from a dictatorial regime. The other groups are still warring among themmselves. Thus the Gurage avoid confrontation, work hard and take care of one another to ensure their well-being and security. They look to their elders for guidance and wisdom.

NOTES

1. Everett E. Hagen, *The Economics of Development* (Homewood, Ill.: Richard D. Irwin, Inc., 1980) 218.

2. Max Weber, *The Protestant Ethic and the Spirit of Capitalism* (London: Charles Scribners Sons, 1930).

3. Everett E. Hagen, *The Economics of Development*, 218.

4. David C. McClelland, *The Achievement Motivation* (New York: Appleton-Century-Crofts, 1953).

5. Everett E. Hagen, *On the Theory of Social Change* (Homewood, Ill.: Dorsey Press, 1962) 309.

6. John Spencer Trimingham, *Islam in Ethiopia* (London: Frank Cass & Co, 1965) 186.

7. Gebreyesus Hailemariam, *The Gurage and their Culture* (New York: Vantage Press, 1991). William A. Shack, *The Gurage: A People of the Enset Culture* (London: Oxford University Press, 1966) 4, 35–37.

8. Gebreyesus Hailemariam, *The Gurage and their Culture*, 2–3.

9. Dinberu Alemu et. al, *Gogot* (Addis Ababa: Artistic Printers, 1987), 108–139.

10. Guebre Sellassie, Vol. 1 quoted in Margery Perham, *The Government of Ethiopia* (Chicago: Northwestern University Press, 1969), 124.

11. Isenberg and Krapt, quoted in William A. Shack, *The Gurage: A People of the Enset Culture.*

12. William A. Shack, *The Gurage: A People of the Enset Culture*, 34, 71, 73.

13. Shack, *The Gurage A People of the Enset Culture,* 78.

14. Gebreyesus Hailemariam, *The Gurage and their Culture*, 30–34.

15. Dinberu Alemu, *Gogot.*

16. Phillip Lebel, "Oral Tradition and Chronicles on Gurage Immigration," in *Journal of Ethiopian Studies, Vol. 12, No. 2 (1974).*

17. William A. Shack, *The Gurage: A People of the Enset Culture,* 27.

18. The kilil policy redefined the Silte as a non-Gurage subgroup (descendants of Arab settlers). This did not make the Gurage hostile towards the Silte. In fact, they applauded the attention their Gurage sub-group was receiving. This information was gathered by the author through interviews.

19. Based on information gathered through interviews.

20. YaGurage Betina Nurow Azagaj Committee, *Guragena Nurow*, (1948) 35.

21. Tesfa Gebreyes, *Aymalal* (Addis Ababa Commercial Printing Press, 1987) 64.

22. Tesfaye Gebreyes, *Aymalal* (Addis Ababa: Commercial Printing Press, 1987) 83.

23. Quoted in Tesfaye Gebreyes, *Aymalal,* 18.

24. Shimelis Bonsa, "Migration, Urbanization and Urban Labor Undertakings: The Case of the Kistane of Addis Ababa C. 1900–1974," Unpublished M. A. Thesis in History, The School of Graduate Studies, Addis Ababa Univeristy (May 1997) 130–131.

25. Based on the author's survey in Addis Ababa.

26. Based on the author's survey.

27. Gebreyesus Hailemariam, *The Gurage and their Culture*, 120. Getinet Assefa, "Indigenous Institutions and Local Development Initiatives: Case Studies from Selected Gurage Areas of Ethiopia," Unpublished M.A. Thesis. Regional and Local Development Studies, Addis Ababa University, (1999) 97 & 98.

28. Getinet Assefa, "Indigenous Institutions and Local Development Initiatives," 98.

29. Gebreyesus Hailemariam, *The Gurage and their Culture,* 119.

30. Based on information gathered through an interview.

31. Based on information gathered through an interview.

32. Based on information gathered through an interview.

33. Kanyazmach Teka Egeno.

34. Gebreyesus Haile Mariam, *The Gurage and their Culture,* 124.

35. Gebreyesus Haile Mariam, *The Gurage and their Culture,* 125.

36. Tesfaye Gebreyes, *Aymalal,* 26.

37. Based on the author's interview.

38. For information on the Soddo see Shimelis Bonsa. "Migration, Urbanization and Urban Labor Undertakings: The Case of the Kistane of Addis Ababa. C. 1900–1974", (May 1997) 100–120

39. Based on information gathered through interviews.
40. Nega Mezlekia, *Notes from the Hyena's Belly* (New York: Picador, 2001) 226–228.
41. Based on information gathered through interviews.
42. Based on an interview with a Gurage entrepreneur.
43. Based on interviews with Gurage entrepreneurs.
44. Based on an interview with a Gurage entrepreneur.
45. Based on information gathered through an interview.
46. YaGurage Betina Nuro Azagaj Committee, 35.
47. Tesfa Gebreyes, *Aymalal,* 66.
48. Based on information gathered through the author's interview with Kanyazmach Teka Egano.
49. See William Schack, *The Gurage: A People of the Enset Culture* (New York: Oxford University Press, 1966) 166–168.
50. See Gebreyesus Haile Mariam, *The Gurage and their Culture*.118.
51. See Worku Nida, "The Revivalist Movement of Hassan Enjamo." Unpublished Essay for a B.A., History Department, Addis Ababa University. (June, 1984).
52. Worku Nida, "The Revivalist Movement of Hassan Enjamo," 4.
53. Worku Nida, 4–5.
54. Worku Nida, 5.
55. See Dinberu Alemu, et. al. *Gogot* (Addis Ababa: Artistic Printers, 1988) 218.
56. Most of the information about Yejoka is taken from Worku Nida, "The Revivalist Movement of Hassan Enjamo" and Dinberu Alemu et. al., *Gogot.*
57. Getinet Assefa, "Indigenous Institutions and Local Development Initiatives: Case Studies From Selecte Gurage Areas of Ethiopia," 63.
58. Based on information gathered through interviews.
59. Based on information gathered through an interview.
60. The words of the late Likatiguhan Getachew Debela.
61. The author was told an interesting story about a father who passed away and left all his property to one of his children because the others did not help him as much when he was alive. The children who were left out of the will brought the case before the elders. The elders decided that the property should be divided among all the children and their mother according to the contribution that each one of them had made to the well-being of the father. They were all satisfied with the decision and went about living their lives.
62. Gebreyesus Hailemariam, *The Gurage and their Culture,* 35.
63. Dinberu Alemu et. al., *Gogot,* 119, 125.
64. Excerpted from Getinet Assefa, "Indigernous Institutions," 69.
65. Tesfa Gebreyes, *Aymalal,* 48.
66. A Gurage businessman told the author the following interesting story. Once someone died without collecting the loans he had made. At the funeral, the eldersen stood up and asked if there were people who owed him money. His debtors stood up and acknowledged their debts.

Chapter Three

Summary and Conclusion

Economic development is achieved when there is a widespread and steady improvement in the standard of living of a given society. This requires that more and more people adopt an entrepreneurial attitude, engaging in wealth creation. The Industrial Revolution that transformed Great Britain and the rest of the Western world is attributable largely to the efforts of entrepreneurs. The spread of the new technology would not have been possible without entrepreneurs, who saw profit adapting the new technology to their respective countries. The work of some entrepreneurs in the United States resulted in the creation of higher quality machines that led to its own industrial revolution.

At the time of the Industrial Revolution the interest of the enterprising middle class was equated with the interest of the modern nation-state. The peasantry was allowed to own land and move freely, seeking work and investment opportunity. Markets were unified and merchants moved freely to sell their goods and invest in production. All individuals, groups and interests enjoyed equal citizenship, the freedom to choose their occupations and the right to accumulate wealth. The nation-state promoted commercial agriculture, manufacture and free trade.

Governments in the developed societies played varying roles in promoting industrialization. The interventions in Great Britain, the United States of America, France and Germany were not significant. An entrepreneurial class led economic development. In Germany and France government played more role than in Great Britain and the United States of America. In Japan, on the other hand, an enlightened state, worried about falling behind the West, led economic development through the policy of learning-by-doing a backlog of Western technologies.

An alternative to the entrepreneurial system of development was created in the early twentieth century when the former Soviet Union launched a command growth model. Central planning and a gigantic bureaucracy replaced private entrepreneurs. The Soviets achieved remarkable growth rates in a short period of time. Over time the failure of the Soviet system to compete with the information-intensive economies of the West triggered a change in policy to restructure the economy. The People's Republic of China that had copied the growth model of the Soviets also implemented incremental market-oriented reforms. The failure of the Soviet system to compete with the information-intensive economies of the West unleashed freedom movements in Eastern Europe that culminated in the creation of multiparty democracies and market economies to the surprise of Moscow. The changes in formerly Communist countries proved that a command growth model was not an economic system that could enforce persistent technological advance and economic development. The experience of the former Soviet bloc countries and China illustrate that command growth is possible for short periods, even decades, but cannot be sustained for a long period of time.

In the fourth quarter of the twentieth century, four Southeast Asian countries joined the ranks of the industrial societies: South Korea, Hong Kong, Singapore and Taiwan, nicknamed the Four Tigers. The governments of these countries created generous incentives for domestic and foreign entrepreneurs, effectively used foreign aid from the United States of America and exploited export markets to achieve and sustain spectacular growth rates.

With the exception of South Africa, the African continent is still largely untouched by technological advance and economic growth. At the time of the first Industrial Revolution in the eighteenth century, not much was known about Africa. One hundred years later, Africa was still lagging behind without an entrepreneurial class to adapt modern technology. Africa's trade relation with the outside world was weak and harmful. South Africa was the only exception because of its large number of White settlers and strong entrepreneurial class.

In the late nineteenth century, South Africa was a progressive economy capable of internalizing new technology. Today, South Africa has a large and prosperous economy with a sophisticated infrastructure. Because of the legacy of the old Apartheid system, however, South Africa consists of a First World (largely White and Indian) and a Third World (largely Black). A strong entrepreneurial class and the wage system transformed the society, although much of the advance was based on exploiting cheap Black labor. Blacks were denied equal citizenship under Apartheid, but did benefit from the wage system. Ironically, they were able to live in relatively better conditions than the majority of peasant populations in independent Africa.

South Africa, of course, does not fit the African mold. Economic development began in colonial Africa only after the Second World War. Most of the former colonies gained their independence in the late 1950s and early 1960s. Government rather than private entrepreneurship assumed leadership in the business of economic development. The rationale by international development specialists was that the private sector was considered inadequate to carry out the task of industrialization. It was believed that government would achieve industrialization quickly and harmoniously. The approach was appealing to the political elite for the purpose of self-preservation. It was also welcomed by the public because it did not conflict with the largely communal tradition. Yet government could not develop the base for the industrial liftoff and modernization of African countries. The reason is not hard to find. If the private sector is inadequately developed to conduct the business of economic development, so is the government sector. This was amply borne out be experience. African countries that emphasized government control or a socialist model, such as Tanzania fell far behind the market-oriented countries, such as Kenya and Cote d'Ivoire.

At the end of the Second World War, the United States and its Western allies initiated an international assistance mechanism to promote economic development in poor countries. But most of the poor countries, especially in Africa, have become dependent on foreign aid and loans for their survival. It was assumed by the advanced societies that with some outside assistance, development would follow in poor countries. Yet only a handful of countries have joined the ranks of leading industrial countries. These countries were able to achieve economic development because they had an entrepreneurial class that could borrow and adapt modern technology and new ideas.

The experience of Ethiopia has been different from the rest of Africa. Prior to the late nineteenth century its history was one of inter-ethnic (also inter-religious) imperial conquests. Ethiopia exhausted itself fighting internecine wars for centuries. At the time of the second Industrial Revolution Ethiopia was an independent country with a national market. It was, however, undeveloped and did not possess an entrepreneurial class that can adapt modern technology.

In the late nineteenth century, Emperor Menelik opened the country to the West; with the help of foreign entrepreneurs some of the inventions of the modern world came to the country for the first time. The establishment of Addis Ababa (New Flower), the capital city of Ethiopia, and the influx of foreign entrepreneurs created employment opportunities and growth prospects for domestic entrepreneurs. Relying on their experience as skilled artisans, traders and migrant workers, the Gurage, especially Soddo (Kistane) Gurage, provided much of the labor requirements of the city. They accounted for fifty percent of the labor force in Addis Ababa at this time.

The modernization attempt continued in the first phase of the reign of Emperor Haile Selassie in the 1920s, though nothing significant occurred. The Great Depression made it difficult to attract foreign capital. Subsequently, Ethiopia fell victim to the Italian occupation that lasted for five years from 1936 up to 1941. The Italian occupation provided a network of roads that the country had never seen before. But in order to create a monopoly for their merchants, the Italians expelled foreign residents and discriminated against domestic traders and artisans, especially Gurage merchants.

Liberation came to Ethiopia in 1941 and the interest in modernization resumed at the end of the Second World War during the second phase of Haile Selassie's reign (1941-1974). Haile Selassie allied the country with the United States of America; as a result, Ethiopia received generous foreign aid and technical assistance for development. The Government played a leading role in development efforts but the economy remained market-oriented. Modern laws were passed, the Parliament was restored and a free public and university education system was introduced. Haile Selassie, however, failed to liberalize the political process and turn land over to the peasantry.

Ethiopia's increased contact with the West created more opportunities for trade and economic development. Domestic entrepreneurs enjoyed greater opportunity for growth, although the Imperial elite, jealous of their own entrepreneurs, favored foreign residents, such as Greeks, Armenians, Indians and Arabs. In the 1960s and early 1970s, the Gurage entrepreneurs competed successfully against foreign residents and dominated a wide range of businesses in the Markato, the central market in Addis Ababa. They invested some of their profits in commercial agriculture, thereby introducing new ideas and techniques into the countryside.

Upon the overthrow of Emperor Haile Selassie, the Stalinist Regime of Mengistu Hailemariam departed radically from the market economy. Mengistu Hailemariam abolished the Parliament, established a Marxist-Leninist state, allied the country with the former Soviet Union and adopted a command growth model. Land and major industrial and trading activities were "nationalized." The old tenure system was abolished, giving the peasantry temporary relief from onerous obligations, but peasants were not allowed to own land. They still lived as tenants, lacking the pride and security of ownership. They made compulsory deliveries of grain to the state at a fixed price. They were denied the right to sell their labor or move freely to seek work. They were forced into collective farms and further impoverished. They were forcibly drafted into the military service and many perished fighting against Tigrayan rebels in the north.

All the foreign managers and entrepreneurs left the country because of the government's nationalization policy. The government confiscated all private businesses and commercial farms and drove domestic entrepreneurs out of the countryside. The state monopolized trade and manufacturing. The government restricted the free movement of merchants and traders, interregional trade and established its own marketing and import-export monopolies. Consequently, domestic entrepreneurs were forced to flee the country or join the underground economy in order to survive. In the end, the Stalinist regime of Mengistu Hailemariam destroyed the country's productive capacity and starved the society. Another famine worse than that in 1973/74 hit the north and other parts of the country in 1984/85. By 1990, the regime tried to introduce the Gorbachev "third way" reforms.

In 1991, the Stalinist regime of Mengistu Hailemariam was driven out of power by the Tigrayan rebel army from the north. Eritrea split from Ethiopia and the new regime of Meles Zenawi redrew the map of Ethiopia along ethnic lines known as kilil, a divisive policy reminiscent of the Italian period.

All lands still belonged to the state and the government kept its monopoly over leading sectors of the economy. Some of the restrictions imposed on the private sector were lifted and private entrepreneurs got a chance to regroup, although new barriers emerged. Private entrepreneurs had to compete with party-owned businesses that were accorded preferential treatment. Because the kilil policy restricted free movement of labor and capital; most business activities were concentrated in Addis Ababa.

Looking back on the history of Ethiopia's development, one finds that political leaders always rise to state power by amassing military might. Once in power, leaders dominate the rest of the society through military might and appropriate the economic surplus for purposes of pursuing elite status and self-preservation. The political leaders create a government monopoly over the lucrative economy and discriminate against domestic entrepreneurs. The worst form of centralization and repression occurred during the Stalinist regime of Mengistu Hailemariam. Despite all this, however, domestic entrepreneurs, the majority of them Gurage, have worked with resilience and patience and managed to create wealth for themselves and the rest of the society. The Gurage contribute disproportionately to the economic development of Ethiopia. They are just four percent of the population of Ethiopia, yet they account for fifty-five to sixty percent of the business activities in Addis Ababa alone. How do they do this?

Studies have shown that an entrepreneurial attitude is concentrated in a particular social group that is quite different from the rest of the population of a given country. In African countries, for instance, a large number of entrepreneurs come from the Ibo of Nigeria, Luo in Kenya and Gurage in Ethiopia.

Historically, these groups have been hardworking and contributed a major share of the total output of their respective societies.

Several explanations have been given for the origins of entrepreneurial attitude. For Max Weber, the Protestant Ethic is responsible for entrepreneurial behavior while David C. McClelland believes that it is a result of achievement motivation inculcated in early childhood. Everett E. Hagen believes that the effort to discount or overcome derogation of a social group by the rest of the society of the same culture and blood creates an entrepreneurial attitude in that group.

These various theories increase our understanding about the origins of entrepreneurial behavior, but a generalization cannot be made about the origins of entrepreneurship. Each case has to be treated separately. In Ethiopia, for instance, a large number of entrepreneurs come from the Gurage, but no serious study has been done about this. A World Bank study by Taye Mengistae about African ethnic businesses makes a conclusion that Gurage-owned manufacturing businesses in Ethiopia perform better than those owned by other groups. The study ascribes this success to the larger size and faster growth rate of Gurage businesses, but it does not tell us where the entrepreneurial attitude comes from.

The Gurage have a particular mentality. They believe in the dignity of work. They are frugal and invest in productive activities. They cooperate and network among themselves. Yet the Gurage are not racially different from other Ethiopian groups. They have had no colonial or other contact with the West. How did they acquire entrepreneurial behavior while the others did not? The Gurage entrepreneurial attitude could be attributed to their specific history and the socioeconomic institutions that have shaped and sustained such behavior over time.

The Gurage come from the fertile and mountainous region in southwestern Ethiopia. They are mobile and live all over the country, working in a wide range of productive activities. They make up four percent of the Ethiopian population. The Gurage are culturally the same people. They have a common language, spoken in three different dialects of eastern, western and northern Gurage. There are three types of believers among the Gurage: Christians, Muslims and followers of indigenous faiths. Historians and linguists of Ethiopia believe that the Gurage are descendants of Tigrayans from Gur'a (in present-day Akkele Guzay, in Eritrea) and the Sidama. The Amhara mixed with the Gurage and influenced their language and religion. In their history, the Gurage had fought among themselves and had suffered from enemy attacks and enslavement. They had fought against the Oromo, Amhara, Hadya and other Sidama groups.

The Gurage consist of four major subgroups: Ya sabat bet Gurage (Gurage of Seven Houses) in the west, Masqan in the east, Soddo Kistane in the north and Silte in the south. The Chaha, Ezha, Muher, Ennemor, Maqorqor and Engagany make up Ya Sabat bet Gurage Hibret (The Seven Houses of Gurage Cooperation), a peace and unity vow with a judicial system of its own known as Yejoka. The peace and unity vow of all Bete Gurage or Gurage subgroups that was modeled after Yejoka is known as Gogot.

The Gurage have occupied their present territory for centuries. Each Bete Gurage (Gurage subgroup) was organized to the village level under a system called Sera with its own administrative rules and laws. At the top of the Sera was an elected Azmach (Imam for Muslims), meaning chief or king, who enforced the rules and laws, assisted by elders. Although each Bete Gurage had its own Sera, the rules and laws of all the subgroups were and still are similar.

The economy in the Gurage region is based on mixed agriculture and trade. The Gurage are also skilled artisans. The highland areas grow various types of cereals and vegetables. The lowlands grow enset (the main staple plant of the Gurage), coffee, tobacco, chat, cotton, corn and various root crops. The main product of the enset plant is the fermented starch of the pseudo-stem and the corm, known as kocho, the staple food of the Gurage and other Sidama groups. Kocho does not spoil easily and can be stored in the ground for a long time, and used during bad times. Historically, starvation and famine were unknown in Gurage, thanks, in part, to the enset plant.

In addition to farming, the Gurage relied on migrant labor and long distance trade to earn income. Adult males migrated to other places in large numbers during the agricultural off-seasons in search of employment opportunities. The Gurage traded in far off places, traveling on foot. They opened their markets to the Amhara, Sidama, Oromo, Kambata and Janjero. Surrounded by warring groups, which threatened their existence and free movement, the Gurage survived by making pacts, preventing hostilities from taking place within the market area and guaranteeing safe conduct for their traders en route.

The Gurage had conducted their own development and defended their independence before their defeat by the Shawans in the late nineteenth century. They held the Shawans at bay for fourteen years (1875-1889) and it took Menelik of Shawa three expeditions before they were finally defeated and brought under the Ethiopian Empire. The Shawans, not yet wedded to the wage system, imposed the gult (fief) system on the Gurage to maintain themselves; consequently, the Gurage were forced to give up their fertile land and live under onerous obligations. The gult system worsened the problem of land scarcity in Gurage. But the Gurage were able to survive by relying more on their experience of trade and migrant labor. They maintained their indigenous institutions of peace and cooperation for their social and economic interactions. In the subsequent periods, they made economic headway using their work ethic, frugality, cooperation and resilience.

The continued success of the Gurage can be ascribed to their social and economic institutions. The two institutions that are primarily responsible for the Gurage work ethic and frugality are family and community.

The Gurage highly value family and community. Parents raise their children properly, teaching them work ethic and respect. Children see helping their parents and themselves as their primary goal. It is important for them to help their parents and receive their blessing. The community respects such children. To be a good child is to receive the blessing of one's parents.

These values are reinforced by the community that is all-inclusive. The community embraces all its members equally. This gives the individual hope because he/she knows that the community cares about him/her. The community promotes work ethic through mentoring and creating employment opportunities making begging an unacceptable behavior.

Through their hard work and frugality, the Gurage have conquered starvation and famine. They have for centuries been independent. The Gurage had achieved many advances prior to the Shawan imperial conquest in the late nineteenth century. They were able to respond to the challenges and opportunities presented by the imperial incorporation, and forged ahead economically as a result of their entrepreneurial experience. They took advantage of a wider market. Gurage artisans and laborers who were brought as captives to Addis Ababa provided much of the labor needed at the palace workshop. Some of them migrated to Addis Ababa and worked for foreign residents: Greeks, Indians, Yemenites, Armenians and Arabs. Many more engaged in small trading and artisan activities of their own, or in menial jobs in the newly established city of Addis Ababa.

During the establishment of Addis Ababa, the Gurage supplied much of the labor force, working in the construction of roads and houses and various types of service activities. They tended vegetable and fruit gardens in the vicinity of Addis Ababa and supplied most of the produce to the city. They retailed foodstuffs and other products. The Soddo Gurage became the tailors of Addis Ababa. They were also involved in long distance trade in the different parts of the expanded empire, working as commercial agents for the imperial elite.

Before the Italian occupation in the 1930s, the retail industry in Addis Ababa was still dominated by foreign residents. But the Gurage were beginning to own some retail stores, and about half of the trading population of the city was made up of the Gurage. They worked on good terms with the Indian merchants and secured a reliable source of supply of raw materials for the production of shama (local costume). They penetrated the vegetable market, the butchery business, tailoring and textiles trading activities. They produced and distributed leather products.

During the Italian occupation (1936-1941), the Gurage worked in road construction and other menial jobs. The Italians dismantled the palace economy, expelled foreign merchants and discriminated against Gurage merchants to create a monopoly for their merchants. Yet the Gurage survived as a result of their experience in the distribution of foodstuffs and other local products. They made money by trading currency, exchanging the lire for the Maria Theresa.

The Gurage entrepreneurs showed rapid growth after the end of the Second World War during the second reign of Emperor Haile Selassie (1941–1974). They admired and emulated success. They mentored one another successfully and funded new businesses with their own personal savings, through Iqub (a credit cooperative) and with family resources. About fifty percent of funding for new businesses came from personal savings. The Gurage are good savers. They save twenty-five to thirty percent of their income. They became prominent in retail and wholesale trade, import-export businesses, restaurant industry, hotel and motel businesses, furniture industry, and manufacturing of liquor, shoes and other consumer goods as well as metal and glass products. They invested in real estate in Addis Ababa and in commercial farming in the countryside. They acquired modern education and became professionals in a wide range of fields. They served ably in the government bureaucracy, but were largely involved in the private sector running their own businesses.

The Gurage progress faced a major setback during the Stalinist regime of Mengistu Hailemariam (1975-1991). The government confiscated their businesses and threw them in jail. Some of them were used as scapegoats for the government's failed policy and executed publicly. Yet they survived using their customary creativity. They joined the informal market. They purchased goods from government stores and retailed them in their shops. They established a market for government coupons (ayar-ba-yar) where they bought coupons from government officials and sold them at a premium to the general public. They ran an underground currency market, trading in the US dollar.

Upon the collapse of the Stalinist regime in 1991, some of the restrictions on the private sector were removed by the new regime of Meles Zenawi. This gave the Gurage entrepreneurs a chance to regroup. However, they faced new barriers. The government's kilil (ethnic-based policy) hampered free movement of labor and capital. The government still owned all lands and its monopoly over the economy continued. The regime raised business taxes and rents on shopping centers and created party-owned businesses, giving them preferential treatment. The Gurage responded by moving into new and profitable enterprises. They partnered with and bought some of the party-owned businesses.

The government still controls the economy. The kilil policy fragmented the market and denied the Gurage the opportunity to invest in commercial agriculture. Most of their entrepreneurial activities are concentrated in Addis Ababa. Well-educated members of the Gurage community have joined the ranks of entrepreneurs, running key businesses, such as banks, insurance companies, real estate and manufacturing.

If there is one factor that can define the continued success of the Gurage, it is their cooperation. For the Gurage, cooperation is the starting point for everything. Their work ethic, frugality, peace, security and all other virtues flow from their cooperation that they have achieved by creating trust and mutual respect among themselves. Through cooperation, the Gurage have managed to control violence; and consequently, they have been able to direct their energies and resources towards productive pursuits and peaceful manners.

There are a number of institutions that have helped the Gurage build trust and mutual respect. First, there is a caring and loving family, teaching work ethic, respect and sense of community at an early age. An all-embracing community reinforces these values by taking care of one another through Oujo, Idir and mentoring. Sera and Gurda help build friendship, trust and cooperation. Yejoka sets the standards for the social behavior of the Gurage. Yejoka rules prohibit all forms of oral and physical aggression and promote cooperation, mutual respect and kindness toward one another among the Gurage. Elders follow Yejoka rules; settle disputes and keep the peace.

Through their enduring institutions, the Gurage have been able to create a successful commercial community of individual responsibility, economic endeavor and peace. Their experience debunks the long-held notion that useful institutions of development only come from the West. By embracing trade and wage labor on their own, the Gurage have managed to escape the Malthusian population-food dilemma of a precarious subsistence economy and thereby staved off mass starvation and famine. By relying on a private economy rather than government, they have been able to create expanding employment opportunities for themselves and to contribute disproportionately to the economic development of the country.

The Gurage always abide by peace and cooperation as the premise for their economic and social interactions. John P. Powelson, in his seminal work, *Centuries of Economic Endeavor*, rightly said that the ultimate explanation of economic development does not lie in economic resources, such as land, labor and capital or in social factors, such as education and religion. "All these will be added," he said, "when most people learn that it is good business to be just and considerate toward one's neighbors; to solve quarrels peacefully; and to be held accountable for the efficient use of resources."[1]

The Gurage had been victims of internal feuding and external attacks in their history. They were forced to learn peace and cooperation as a matter of survival. By controlling violence and destruction, they were able to direct their energies and resources towards productive activities. When they were brought under the Imperial Ethiopian Government in the late nineteenth century, they had already transitioned to the safer pursuits of trade and wage labor. They continued to rely on their indigenous institutions for their social and economic interactions. All these factors helped them to meet successfully the challenges and opportunities presented by their incorporation into Ethiopian society and to forge ahead economically in the subsequent periods with patience and resilience.

The lessons of Gurage entrepreneurship are quite clear. First, it is difficult if not impossible for any society to achieve economic development unless its members are willing to cooperate to resolve their internal differences and learn to live together in peace, thereby allowing high priority to the goal of economic development. Experience has shown that international assistance has worked well in societies that have relative peace and stability.

Second, the nature of economic production of a given community or society could have an impact on social behavior. Because many poor countries have taken a long time as a subsistence economy, they have developed rigid and inflexible attitudes. By embracing trade and the wage system, the Gurage have learned patience, resilience, compromise, and peace. They are relatively flexible and receptive to new ideas.

Third, experience has shown that societies with a strong entrepreneurial class have been able to adapt modern technology fairly quickly. On the other hand, poor countries, the majority of them in Africa, are getting poorer, lacking an entrepreneurial group, and unable to adapt modern technology. Yet these societies have successful entrepreneurial communities they can emulate and adapt modern technology. There is a lot to be learned in this regard from the Gurage history and the socioeconomic institutions that have shaped and sustained the successful Gurage entrepreneurship over a long period of time.

NOTE

1. John P. Powelson, *Centuries of Economic Endeavor* (Ann Arbor: The University of Michigan Press, 1997) 3.

Appendix I

Case Study

Kenyazmach Teka Egeno The Quintessential Entrepreneur & The First Recipient of the Haile Selassie Prize Trust Award in Agriculture

I was born in 1919, according to the Ethiopian Calendar at a place called Yillie, five kilometers east of Butajara. I come mainly from Maskan and Soddo Gurage subgroups. I am also part Silte.

I lived in Yillie until I was eight years old. The neighborhood where I grew up consisted of different Gurage subgroups, such as Maskan, Silte and Soddo (Dobi, Damwie, Wogara, and Wachu). They all lived together under the same laws and rules.

I left my hometown in 1934 when I was fifteen years old for Addis Ababa. I first worked as a street vendor, selling sugar cane and small articles. I then opened in 1942 a liquor store in Jimma with 900 bottles of alcoholic drinks that I purchased on credit for a dollar a piece from a Greek distillery in Addis Ababa.

The Greek owner, Kosta, gave credit to many retailers like me. But most of them did not honor their commitment. I kept my word and paid my account on time. Unfortunately, this made Kosta nervous. At this time, in Jimma, there were only six well-established merchants: 3 Greeks, 1 Armenian, 1 Turkish, and 1 Tigrayan (from Eritrea). I had nothing compared to these merchants. I did not even have nine dollars in my pocket when I took nine hundred dollars worth of liquor on credit.

While retailing liquor, I started to study if there is a market in Jimma for other goods that may be profitable. Thus, I asked the komarit (the women tej bar owners) if they would like me to bring them shoes from Addis Ababa (etiyie, chama lamtalotwoy kaddis ababa? Wuy, aferyiblany, ishi). They welcomed the idea with great enthusiasm. I then took measurements of their feet on paper and went to Addis Ababa to a friend of mine who was a cobbler and placed the orders. I requested shiny uppers for the shoes that could easily be dusted off.

A partial view of Butajara, Soddo, Gurage

The shoe business took off so fast that I became famous in Jimma. The women now came with a long list of items that they wanted me to bring from Addis Ababa, such as, hand-operated flour mills, tej barrels, and so on. I became a major player in the business community; and consequently, the foreign businesses that had been prominent since the late nineteenth century were slowly declining. By this time, I had already saved thirteen thousand dollars.

My struggle, however, with Kosta, my Addis Ababa supplier of liquor, was not over. I once made a suggestion about the label on the liquor bottle. He thought I was trying to cheat him. He cursed at me (gushasha Gurage, yitabatunow) and told me to go away. I asked him, "Why do you curse at me? Why do you call my father names? I paid you on time. I was just trying to help." He had once had me thrown in jail because I noticed a residue in the liquor and suggested that I could clean it for him. He thought I was trying to cheat him and got me arrested. A powerful, savvy lawyer who was a good friend of mine got me out. He came to the police station with two horses, one for me and one for him. We both rode home from the police station.

The Greek distiller apologized for the whole incident and gave me one more shipment on credit. I paid him on time again. My promptness never made him comfortable. As the winter season set in, the roads became bad to send shipments to Jimma. Business was slow and I could not place orders as before. He became worried and told me all of a sudden that I was not welcomed at his place again. I knew he was looking for a reason to get rid of me. I told him that I would not set foot at his place again. I was afraid that he might get me thrown in jail if he knew that I had saved money. In those days, ferenj, the white man, was God. To divert his attention, I purposely told him that I did not have any money and asked him if he could spare me some change for my dinner that night.

I then purchased with my own money one truckload of liquor and two truckloads of wine to be sent to Agaro and left for Agerbet, (my hometown) so that he would not bother me. The drivers were instructed to park in front of his distillery as a display. When the Greek owner saw the trucks, he asked where the shipment was heading. They told him that the shipment was heading to Agaro. "Who is there in Agaro?" He asked. They replied, "Teka Egeno." He asked again, "Who gave him this?" They replied, "Who has more money these days? Teka Egeno, or you?" He was mad, and when I got back from my trip three days later, he asked his friends to get us together. He apologized again and gave me $1,200 to buy a suit. I had never worn a suit in my life.

After we made peace, I ordered two more truckloads of drinks before the other three trucks returned to Addis Ababa. He now wanted to enter the

Kanyazmach Teka Egeno

Jimma market and brought in his own Greek retailer there. I told him that I welcomed the competition.I gave him part of the money on the second shipment while he was in Jimma and the balance owing was $5,000.

His Jimma retailer turned out to be an avid gambler. One day he needed money for his gambling and asked me to pay the $5,000 while he was gambling with his friends. I told him that I had only $50 in my pocket and would bring the balance in the afternoon. He quickly snatched the $50 from my hand and gave me a receipt for it. He wrote the number 5 with three zeros without putting a dot after the first zero; and consequently, the receipt read as $5,000 instead of $50.00. Now I decided to hide from him. I took the receipt and flew to Addis Ababa to see Kosta, his boss. I paid $49 for the air ticket. When I arrived at Kosta's, I said, "Kosta, I would like to have my promissory note back. I have already paid the $5,000 to your representative in Jimma. Here is the proof." I gave him the receipt that I brought with me. He wanted to ask me first about his agent. "What does Orestabro do there?" He asked. "He gambles his heart out with his buddies," I answered. "I do not know. When I saw him last, he was sweating badly. I think he lost money," I added. He said, "Ores is useless. I am finished now. I cannot even enjoy what God has given me. He throws my money away. You are the only one who paid me." He was very sad.I told him to take it easy and asked him to pay me back only the $50 that I paid Ores and the $49 that I paid for my ticket. I told him that I came to Addis Ababa to save him. He was very grateful and asked me to be his business partner.

After Kosta, there was no one standing my way. I became too tough to beat. I became the major (if not the only) liquor, beer and wine distributor and owned a Coca-Cola franchise in Jimma. I owned hotels and invested in a coffee plantation. I became the first recipient of the Haile Selassie I Prize Trust Award in Agriculture. However, most of my businesses were later confiscated by the Stalinist Regime of Mengistu Hailemariam. I have been rebounding in the last ten to fifteen years. My present passion is establishing a plant (the author was given a tour) that manufactures ceiling and wall materials from synthetic substances to save trees. I also have a great interest in sharing my experience to improve the quality of Ethiopian coffee across the board. As you can see, however, I am now an old man. I will turn 80 on Nehasie 19, 1999. My sight, teeth, hands and legs have already betrayed me. The only soldiers that are still with me are my tongue, heart and brain.

Appendix II

Case Study

Legesse Zerihun—Chief Executive Director— Waryt Mulutila International, PLC

I was born and raised in Addis Ababa. My parents were grain merchants and owned a flour mill in the Markato, Addis Ababa's central market.

I come from a family of four children (three girls and one boy). I lost my father when I was young. My mother and grandparents raised us. My older sister Tadelech Zerihun and I were given the opportunity to go to school, while my other two sisters had to help with the family business.

My sister Tadelech subsequently entered the business world herself while I continued with my studies. She was in the berbere business and became one of the well-known distributors in the country. I helped the family during my spare times, but my mother and sisters were the breadwinners of the family. They were hardworking people and I learned the value of work from them.

I grew up in a loving and respectful family. There was no rivalry among us; we had nothing to fight over; our only goal was to work and survive. We helped one another and treated our mother and grandparents with deference and respect.

My mother and my sister Tadelech had great influence on me while I was growing up. My mother was a woman of great integrity. Relatives and friends used to deposit their savings and valuables with her. People used to bless my mother for her honesty and service. My mother was a respected woman. This was one of the values that I learned from her. There were times when she fed the workers in our house first before she fed us. She was always fair and never rushed to judgment. I remember that I was once involved in a scuffle with a neighborhood boy and people were watching while we were slugging it out and did nothing to stop it. My mother saw what was going on as she was passing by. She did not come to my help, as most mothers would probably had done. Instead, she asked the people who were watching why they did not break up the fight and create peace. I was angry with my mother because she did not come to my assistance. I refused to go back home that day. However, our neighbors respected my mother for her sense of justice. I understood after I grew up why my mother did not come to my assistance.

The other major influence on me was my sister Tadelech. She used to work fourteen to sixteen hours a day to support us. Her day always began at 5 in the morning. It is because of her that all of us are here today. She taught me the value of work and love of family. She has been more than a sister to me. I have always looked up to her. She is a successful woman now and lives well here in Addis Ababa. She is a role model to all of us. I have used her lessons of hard work, independence and perseverance to run my own business today with my wife, children and other employees. My wife and I have always made sure that our children learned the value of work. We used to make them wash our cars for stipends. I remember that one of our children did not like to soil his hands with dirt, so I created incentives to encourage him to practice pottery.

We also believe in education. We have four children, two boys and two girls. Our two older children (a girl and a boy) hold graduate degrees in business. Our younger son is a college graduate and our younger daughter is finishing her undergraduate work in marketing. She has a talent for crafts and supports herself making jewelry from beads. One of my boys is musically inclined and used to work in a popular band here in town while studying. We support our children to pursue their own dreams.

When we opened our business, we made our children start from the lowest level, cleaning cars at our service station, working as messengers, office clerks and as porters in the furniture department. They identified themselves with the company by their job titles as a clerk, a messenger, or a porter. We did not give them a free ride just because they are our children. Our older daughter and older son are now department managers in our company. They report to the general manager who is not a family member.

A work ethic and mutual respect are important values in our family and the whole Gurage community. We trust and respect our elders because they are our protectors. We listen to their advice and respect their decisions even when we think that they may not be in our own self-interest.

Appendix III

Case Study

Lemma Habtegiorgis—Chairman, Nib Bank

I was born in 1939, according to the Ethiopian Calendar in Ezha, Sabat-bet Gurage. I stayed there until I was 5 and then moved to Dire Dawa to live with my older brother where I completed my elementary and high school education. I can say that I am a Dire Dawan.

My brother was employed in domestic services and his income was small. I had to work part-time jobs to support myself while going to school. After completing high school, I joined the Commercial Bank of Ethiopia in Addis Ababa and pursued my college education in the evening for two years. Subsequently, I enrolled in an external degree program with an American university and earned a law degree.

After two and half years with the Commercial Bank, I joined the United Nations and worked in Ibadan, Nigeria for three years. While at Ibadan, I earned my BBA and MBA degrees through the same external degree program. I left the UN at 52 (under a deferred retirement plan) after many years of service. My wife (also from Ezha) and I then focused more on our own private business.

My wife is a nurse by training. She began running our business (importing and distributing children's products) while I was still working at the UN. We have now expanded the business, (The Twins, established in 1990), and added other undertakings—restaurants and a supermarket. I also formed along with my friends a micro financing business called Agar. We created Nib Bank and Nib Insurance Company. I served initially as a board member in all three organizations, and was later elected Chairman of the Bank, having served five years as a board member. I now work in the Bank only and have given up my posts at the other two organizations to avoid conflict of interest.

There are business opportunities in the country today, but certain problems still remain. A major issue that is facing the Ethiopian economy and the banking industry is the question of privatization. I do not believe in government monopoly. I am a strong believer in privatization. The role of government should be to provide security and socioeconomic infrastructure. The Government should not involve itself in business activities.

The economy should be privatized, including land ownership for both internal and external organizations. Land has to enter the free market and commercial farms have to be promoted. This is how Ethiopian entrepreneurs can grow. This is how the brain drain can stop and outside entrepreneurs can work in joint venture with Ethiopian entrepreneurs.

The urban decay we are now seeing in most parts of Addis Ababa is due to government involvement in the housing industry. Private homes are maintained properly while state-owned houses and buildings are run-down. The government should sell these houses to the tenants or the general public and get out of the housing industry entirely. The Government cannot run the housing business efficiently. It should focus, instead, on the infrastructure of Addis Ababa and the rest of the country.

We live in an era of information technology; institutions of higher learning have to be prepared to meet the challenges of the information economy. However, there is a major concern in the business community regarding the quality of Ethiopia's higher education. While the increase in the number of public and private colleges is encouraging, the inadequate qualifications of college graduates is worrisome.

Private banking is an exciting and challenging undertaking in an era of rapid globalization. Of course, globalization has not fully entered Ethiopia yet. The discussion around the banking industry today is whether joining the World Trade Organization (WTO) is beneficial to Ethiopia. There are two views on this subject. One is that global competition will drive us out of business completely. The other view, which I support, is that we are part of the world, and globalization will benefit us; we will, as a result, be an efficient and competitive society. I believe that unless international finance enters the country, we cannot develop with internal resources alone. Whatever the cost, we have to think in terms of globalization. International banking and financial institutions as well as telecommunication enterprises have to freely enter the country so that there will be a transfer of modern technology to the country. The long run benefits of globalization will outweigh the short run costs. In the long run, globalization will make us economically strong and successful. The current government has not fully embraced globalization yet. But globalization is rapidly integrating the world economy. Whether we like it or not, five or ten years from now, we will be more global citizens than just Ethiopians.

Bibliography

Abir, Mordechai, *Ethiopia: The Era of the Princes:* New York: Praeger Publishers, 1968.
Africa Institute of South Africa, *Africa at a Glance,* 1992 and 1995/6.
Africa Report, "The Politics of Foreign Assistance," May–June, 1980.
Alemu, Dinberu et. al., *Gogot,* Addis Ababa: Artistic Printers, 1987.
Assefa, Getinet, "Indigenous Institutions and Local Development Initiatives: Case Studies from Selected Gurage Areas of Ethiopia," Unpublished M.A. Thesis, Regional and Local Development Studies, Addis Ababa University, 1999.
Bauer, P. T., Reality and Rhetoric: Studies in the Economics of Development, Cambridge: Harvard University Press, 1984.
Bonsa, Shimelis, "Migration, Urbanization and Urban Labor Undertakings: The Case of the Kistane of Addis Ababa, 1900–1974," Unpublished M.A. Thesis in History, The School of Graduate Studies, Addis Ababa University, May 1997.
Doresse, Jean, *Ethiopia,* London: Elek Books Ltd., 1956.
Gebreyes, Tesfa, *Aymelel,* Addis Ababa: Commercial Printing Press, 1987.
Goldman, Marshall I., *USSR in Crisis: The Failure of an Economic System,* New York: W.W. Norton & Company, 1983.
Gruhl, Max, *Abyssinia at Bay,* London: Hurst and Blackett Ltd., 1933.
Hagen, Everett E., *The Economics of Development,* Homewood, Ill.: Richard D. Irwin, Inc., 1980.
Hailemariam, Gebreyesus, *The Gurage and their Culture,* New York: Vantage Press, 1991.
Hogendorn, Jan S. *Economic Development,* New York: Harper and Row, Publishers, 1987.
Houn, Franklin W. *A Short History of Chinese Communism,* Englewood Cliffs, New Jersey: Prentice Hall, Inc., 1973
International Monetary Fund, *Press Release,* No. 96/51.
Jones and Monroe, *A History of Ethiopia,* Oxford: Oxford University Press, 1935.

Lebel, Phillip, "Oral Tradition and Chronicles on Gurage Immigration," *Journal of Ethiopian Studies,* Vol. 12, No. 2, 1974.
Lewis, Herbert, "A Reconsideration of the Socio-Political Systems of the Western Galla," *Journal of Semetic Studies,* Vol. 9, No. 1, Spring 1964.
Loehr, William and John P. Powelson, *The Economics of Development and Distribution,* New York: Harcourt Brace Jovanovich, Inc., 1981.
Lyne, Tamrat, "Ethiopia's Transitional Period Economic Policy Draft," Nehassie 1983.
McClelland, David C. *The Achievement Motivation,* New York: Appleton-Century-Crofts, 1953.
Meier, Gerald M. and Robert E. Baldwin, *Economic Development: Theory, History, Policy,* Huntington, New York: Robert E. Publishing Company, 1976.
Myrdal, Gunnar, *Rich Lands and Poor: The Road to World Properity,* New York: Harper and Row, 1957.
Nida, Worku, "The Revivalist Movement of Hassan Enjamo," Unpublished Essay for a B.A., History Department, Addis Ababa University, June 1984.
Nove, Alec, *An Economic History of the USSR,* Baltimore: Penguin Books, 1975.
Pankhurst, Richard, *Economic History of Ethiopia, 1800–1935,* Addis Ababa: Haile Selassie I University Press, 1968.
Perham, Margery, *The Government of Ethiopia,* Evanston: Northwestern University Press, 1969.
Powelson, John P., *Centuries of Economic Endeavor,* Ann Arbor: The University of Michigan Press, 1997.
Prebish, Paul. "Commercial Policy in the Underdeveloped Countries," *American Economic Review,* May 1959.
Rodney, Walter, *How Europe Underdeveloped Africa,* Washington, D.C.: Howard University Press, 1982.
Salvatore, Dominick, *International Economics,* New York: Mcmillian, 1993.
Sertoader, 29 Yekatit 1982.
Shack, William C., The Gurage: A People of the Enset Culture, London: Oxford University Press, 1966.
Snow, Edgar, *Red China Today,* New York: Random House, 1970.
Teferra, Daniel, "Performance of Ethiopia's Socialist Economy," A Discussion Roundtable in Ethiopia, The Orkand Corporation, Silver Spring, MD., 9 November 1989. "Ethiopia: Post-Cold War Market Reform and Globalization," *Pan-Ethiopia Forum,* Volume 2, Issue 1, 2000–2001.
The Economist, 6 May 1995.
The Margin, Vol. 3., No. 1, September 1987.
The World Bank, *World Development Report,* 1989 & 1997.
Todaro, Michael P. *Economic Development,* New York: Longman, 1994.
Trimingham, John Spencer, *Islam in Ethiopia,* London: Frank Cass & Co., 1965.
Walton, Gary M. and Ross W. Robertson, *History of the American Economy*, New York: Harcourt Brace Jovanovich, Inc., 1983.
Weber, Max, *The Protestant Ethic and the Spirit of Capitalism,* London: Charles Scribners Sons, 1930.
YaGurage Betina Nurow Azagaj Committee, *Guragena Nurow,* 1948.

Index

Abba Gomol, 18
Abba Jifar, 18
Adal, 13
Adere, 14
Addis Ababa, 51, 65
Ahmad ibn Ibrahim Al-Ghazi, 13, 14
Alaba, 10
Amhara, 12, 13
Arsi, 11, 17
Aussa, 14
Australia, 1
Axum, 7

Bale, 11, 16
Belgium, 1
Bete Israel, 9
Borana, 11, 17

Canada, 1
China, 3, 64
Coffee, 24, 25, 28–30
Command growth, 3
Cote d'Ivoire, 4–5

Damot, 7
Dawaro, 11, 16
Dire Dawa, 25

Enarea, 11, 12, 17
Eritrea, 23–24

Fatagar, 11, 16
France, 1–2, 63

Gama-Moras, 19
Gera, 17–18
Germany, 1–2, 63
Goma, 17–18
Gondar, 15
Great Britain, 1–2, 63
Gudru, 19
Gugsa Marsa, 20–21
Gult, 27, 44–45
Guma, 17–18

Hadya, 10–11
Hagen, Everett E., 41, 68
Haile Selassie, 21, 27–29, 45, 52, 66
Harar, 14, 16, 24–25, 27
Hong Kong, 3, 64

Ifat, 9, 11
Industrial Revolution, 1
International Monetary Fund (IMF), 6, 28, 33–35

Japan, 1–2, 63
Jimma, 17–19

Kafficho, 11–12, 17
Kambata, 10
Karayu, 17
Kenya, 5

Lakamt, 17
Lasta, 7
Leka, 17
Leka Kellem, 19
Leka Lekemti, 19
Leka Sayo, 19
Lijj Iyasu, 21
Limmu, 17
Limmu-Enarea, 18

Manz, 12
McClelland, David C., 41, 68
Mecha, 17
Meles Zenawi, 33, 45, 53, 67
Menelik, 24, 65
Mengistu Hailemariam, 29, 33, 45, 52, 66–67
Muhammad Abdullah, 15

New Zealand, 1
Nonno, 17–19

Oromo, 14–17

Parliament, 27–28, 66

Raya, 19
Russia, 2

Sidama, 10
Singapore, 3, 64
Somali, 17
South Africa, 4, 64
South Korea, 3, 64
Soviet development model, 2, 64–65
Sweden, 1
Switzerland, 1

Taiwan, 3, 64
Tambaro, 10
Tanzania, 5
Tewodros, 22
Tulama, 11

Umar Baksa, 10
Umar Shaikh, 26
United States of America, 1–2, 28–29, 63, 66

Wallaga, 11
Wallo, 19
Weber, Max, 41, 68
Wolayta, 11

Yejoka, 43, 57–58
Yeju, 19
Yodit, 9
Yohannes, 22

Zagwe, 9
Zega, 12
Zeila, 12